A STUDENTS WORK FOR C STUDENTS

LUKE PICKETT

ISBN: 1453719008
ISBN-13: 9781453719008

DEDICATION

To Annie, Maddie, Jake, Dennis, and Sophie

TABLE OF CONTENTS

FOREWORD

The emperor has no clothes.

The story goes like this: a con artist claiming to be a magical tailor comes to a kingdom looking to make it rich. He sells the emperor the idea that his special clothes are fabulous and the emperor should pay a lot for them. Of course the tailor is a liar, pretends to put invisible clothes on the emperor, and...oohhhs and ahhhs...the con man tells the emperor the new creations are beautiful. Too embarrassed not to see the clothes don't actually exist, the emperor buys in. The sick lie continues as the king's court does the same...then the entire kingdom. Everyone is too afraid to stray from the acceptance of the majority. Everyone is afraid— except a little child at the annual kingdom parade who shouts out: "The emperor has no clothes!"

Be the little child that sees.

PREFACE

This book is intentionally short because I want teenagers to read it. This is not an anti-education or anti-intellectualism book. The intent of this book is to help kids see education for what it really should be about, because chances are, no one has ever told them why they are even in school—really.

Above all else, I should state here that I am writing about life and not delivering a PhD thesis intended to secure a job in the education industry. In fact, as will become apparent early in the book, the views expressed here are largely opposed within the education industry. The views expressed in this book derive their validation from my own experiences being educated as an A student in both public and private schools, my lifelong observations of my classmates and friends and their life successes, and my voluminous reading and observation of educational philosophy and practices that surround our children today.

I fully expect the vast majority of educational professionals to strongly disagree with many views expressed in this book. And to the extent business owners happen to pick this book up, I hope they will find it highly amusing—and true. The observations expressed here are not intended to insult anyone, but rather to suggest that our education system may be causing some unintended harm to both A students and C students.

Here is the new (draft) vision statement of a regional school district where I live in New Hampshire. From my observations, the ideals expressed in this statement are not a-typical:

"To provide a rigorous and comprehensive education that will prepare our graduates for diverse post-secondary educational opportunities, a collaborative workplace, and active civic participation."

Compare that statement to something like this:

We seek to prepare all students with a strong academic foundation necessary to think independently in a logical and rational manner; to be able to pursue additional education, gainful employment, or his or her own business or vocation—but above all else, to see and embrace the opportunities that face them every day to better themselves and those around them. We seek to educate problem solvers that will endeavor to create opportunity from the risks they encounter rather than allow those risks to limit their hopes and dreams.

It is the viewpoint of this book that while our American education system means well, its goals are vague. It is the intent of this book to instead cast light on the necessity of our system to embolden our children to embrace opportunities for themselves and to use the education system to work hard toward self-realization within a risky world—and not blindly accept what the system says they ought to do.

INTRODUCTION

The next time your high school has a mid-day dismissal, which is quite often these days, I suggest you borrow your mom or dad's car and drive to the two or three (or ten) local, not national, businesses you think are the most successful or your family uses the most. Go in and tell the sales person at the cash register or the front desk that you are a high school student not asking for a job but would like to ask the owner one simple question. When the owner comes out (it will be a little while because she or he is busy making money), tell him or her that you read a book about the success of C students in America. And you want to know what his or her class rank was in high school.

The owner will hesitate...look away...smile...and laugh.

And after you have visited all of the businesses you wanted to see—even the largest locally or regionally owned employers—pick the one you like the best. And then go back and ask that owner for a commission only sales job for next summer. You'll get the job. And you'll get the dream.

The foundation of the American Dream, and indeed the American economy, is built on small business. And the owner of the American small business was more often than not a C student in high school. According to the Small Business Administration's web page, there are almost thirty million small businesses in America, defined as companies with less than five hundred employees, and only about twenty thousand companies above that employee count. If you are one of the lucky ones that don't chase the honor roll sham, then you may be on your way to true success in these United States.

In America today, we as a society have become a herd. We act like a herd in almost everything we do. We buy the same clothes, listen to the same music, like the same movies. And we chase the same goals. Like getting As in school and trying to go to the best colleges. And based on my twenty-eight years in the workplace, it is my judgment that such goals are largely overrated. That's not to say people that get As in school and go to top colleges don't get great jobs and live in really nice houses, drive really nice cars, and make lots of money. They do. Lots of them. But the reality is most people cannot—and should not—chase the almighty A in school and try to attend a top college. Because a) most of us are average academically, and b) America was not built by A students.

A students might tell you a new America is being built by A students, but I believe that's a lie. As we look at our economy in 2009 and 2010, have we in fact built a better America? Did really smart people on Wall Street build something great? Something better? Or to a large extent, have we wandered away from the basics that made this country great? America's strong economic foundation is built upon small businesses. And starting and running a small business means seeing an opportunity, understanding risk, taking that risk, and then managing the risk. And the risk takers in America have historically been average students. That's right...C students start and build most of the job-creating businesses in this country. And what's more, they hire A students to be their attorneys, accountants, and doctors. But it takes the risk taker to start it all, to embrace risk as opportunity, to build a company, to make America the land of opportunity that it is.

This book, therefore, is a challenge to the average student in America—the C student. Will you reject what the system is selling and choose a path that will most likely bring you success in life? This means hard work for you and the goals you set instead of the external goals of the education system. Are you ready?

I. THE PROBLEM:
Chasing the Almighty A

Well…shouldn't *every* student aspire to be an honor roll student? After all, isn't everyone an A student in something?

Nope.

CHAPTER 1:

THE SYSTEM AND MEDIOCRITY

The most successful people I know from high school were C students when we were in school. The most successful people I know today on the Seacoast of New Hampshire tell me they were average students in high school and college—that they barely made it through school. And it's my bet the same statement is true in most communities across this great country. They barely made it through school, but they work for themselves today. They started and now run successful companies, many of them quite large. They are major regional beer manufacturers, major retailers with more than three hundred stores, insurance agents, real estate owners that own and manage thousands apartments nationally, and bakery chain owners. Sure, they went to college. But they had something else...they sensed something else. Their gut told them that the academic world was artificial and its external goals not right for them.

I went to a Catholic all boys high school, so look-ing back, the education system's claim of academic achievement as the end all was a little like the priests telling us about being married. There was an agenda, but without a real understanding or real life experience. Not that the teachers weren't well intended. They were...and they are. But the C students seemed to have almost a sixth sense that the school world is an artificial world early on, and those C students set out to use that artificial academic world for their own benefit instead of accepting the system's identified goals and virtues.

In 2000, I started the New Hampshire division of the most successful real estate company in Maine. Our growth was not as we had expected in our business plan, and the owner confronted me on my lack of progress. Frustrated, I blurted out, "Starting from scratch in a new market is hard! The competition doesn't want us there and is doing everything it can to stop us from gaining a foothold."

The owner of the real estate company and hundreds of thousands of square feet of commercial property just stared at me. He did not blink. Then he said in a calm voice, "Hard? This is hard?"

The owner was a former U.S. Marine Corps helicopter pilot in Vietnam. He was right. Building a business in New Hampshire in 2000 was almost a joke in terms of degree of difficulty compared to truly difficult experiences such as flying wounded soldiers out of a combat zone—or just trying to survive in most of the rest of the world today. I was forty years old and had never really confronted reality. I had been drifting through what I thought was success, always having a good job, pleasing my boss. But those words smacked me in the face. Obviously I hadn't really learned anything about what it takes to be successful or that my incorrectly perceived sense of success in the working world started with academic success in school.

What if I was to say that the American education system—public and private—is ripping off both top students and average students by establishing a system based upon the wrong goals? For average students, the system intentionally teaches them the incorrect goal of pursuing good grades. That somehow success in life will come if only they can achieve better grades and make the honor roll. And as insidious as that misperception is, the system is also hurting top students by unintentionally teaching them to be risk averse. But more on that horrible practice later in the book.

First, let's think about how a classroom is viewed from the perspective of achievement. No matter what terminology is used, a class is typically made up of a few below average students, a bunch of average students, and a few above average students. But "below average" or "average" or "above average" in *what*? Average in knowledge of high school history? Of one's recollection of the personality traits of the major characters in *The Scarlet Letter?* Of memorization of the periodic tables in chemistry?

Is *that* what school is all about? Being better than average—or a lot better than average—at *that* stuff? Really??

No. That's not what educating a young mind is all about.

But that's what the school *system* is all about. Just as most bureaucracies are set up to perpetuate themselves, the school system *sells* something. And what it *says* it sells and what it *actually* sells is very different. If you ask an educator what the business of a school system is, he or she will tell you "education, learning, knowledge, etc." But what the education system is really selling is the grade of A. That's right. The simple letter A, or a numerical grade of 90 to 100. Whether or not a student really earns that A. They are selling the *perception of being above average*—the inference by students and their parents that their performance in school was better than most. Study hard...and be above average.

And from that perspective every subject is taught. All students are lined up behind that perfect score of A in descending order. Of course, if all kids are properly challenged, a small percentage should get As and Bs, the majority of kids should get Cs as they are in the middle as the scores are tallied, and then the scores should tail off again as the rest of the pack pulls up the rear.

This line of thinking is usually okay so long as we are all honest about what we are trying to do. But no one is being honest today, especially our school systems. Think about how we begin our young careers in sports. We all want to be the pitcher in softball or baseball (or most of us do) or be the quarterback in football. But natural talent places some of us in right field or along the offensive line. And what's the matter with that? Some of the greatest baseball and football players of all time played right field or offensive line respectively. But they never would have achieved success in life if their coaches insisted everyone have equal time pitching or throwing passes. Yet that's what we do in our education system. Despite knowing that a whole lot of kids will never get *real* As in geometry or chemistry, we stick to the mode of pushing everyone to keep trying to be an A student in something...any- thing...insisting all kids chase that holy grail of high grades.

So what's wrong with that? The pitchers and quarterbacks are always the heroes in their respective sports, aren't they? Sure they are. So are our brain surgeons and rocket scientists. Yes, we need them. We as a society need brain surgeons and rocket scientists like we need oxygen because we cannot progress without them. The problem is the educational system tells *all of us* to go out there every day and yearn to be A students when most of us won't be A students—ever. But the education system simply cannot deal with that reality. So it takes wild and frequently changing attempts at avoiding the natural result that the majority of kids will end up in the middle. Ironically, by trying *not* to be discouraging, the system creates its own problem of massive discouragement.

Why does the education system do this? Here's the weak foundation that our education system is based upon: If someone gets good grades then good things will happen. Self-esteem will be raised, real achievement will occur, and success in life will soon follow.

So good grades translate into doing well in life.

When was that ever universally true? *Ever?* Sadly, the education system has it backwards: grades *reflect* something, they don't *cause* something. And grades often simply reflect that *some kids are really good at doing school.*

And being really good at school may or may not translate into success later in life. But the education system is stuck on something that is fundamentally false: if everyone was an honor roll student then the world would be a better place. So the system sets its bureaucratic heart on something false...and it therefore fails most of our kids—miserably.

Here is just one example: A local school district where I live in New Hampshire stopped labeling its lowest level class (AP, honors, college prep, etc.). College admissions departments were therefore left to guess the significance of an A in junior year history class. An inference from this strategy can be made that it's an attempt to trick colleges into thinking a high grade in an unlabeled class is worth more than it really is. Just accept the student on meaningless facts—and he will then succeed.

Thirty or forty years ago, the kids sitting on the belly of the bell curve (the C students) understood this simple concept that the honor roll wasn't for everyone. And it wasn't sugar coated. Teachers and most adults would point out reality: "Kid, you are not now, nor are you ever going to be, an honor roll student...so think of something else to grab onto."

And that simple directness, that reality without harshness, set in motion much of the greatness that America still has today. The realization that *everyone is not an honor roll student,* that school isn't everything, actually made America great.

But not now. We are all caught up in the hero syndrome, the self-esteem game, and the belief that somehow academic achievement is a prerequisite for success in life. We all hear about the big stories about the quarterbacks and the pitchers and the MIT or Harvard kids starting Internet companies. Barak Obama became president because he's smart. But really, how many of those super-hero stories are there? Answer: not many. And how many CEOs of Fortune 500 companies are there? Answer: five hundred. But how many small businesses are there? Answer: almost thirty *million*. And how many of those small businesses around your town were started by average students? Answer: most of them.

The American education system *used* to promote the average student getting savvy in ways other than classroom work. Street smart. Common sense. Oh, so corny. Recognizing that one particular path was not the best for most people was simply a logical and natural course of events back then, a course that produced greatness in roles *other than great students*. Like starting a business in a local community that America is actually built upon. But not today. Now the system fears for the self-esteem of that average student. Fears of the moment when that average student realizes the honor roll is unattainable. Fears of that moment because the system has set itself up for failure—the only thing important according to that education system is good grades. The only way to be successful is by getting good grades. The only way to advance is to value what the system values: good grades. How sad. And how dead wrong.

How sad and dead wrong for our children today to be subjected to this blind loyalty to the almighty A. So much so that the system today now pays kids for As in some parts of the country. And if a child doesn't deserve one, well, the system just gives him one... you know...to make him feel better. Schools now have ten valedictorians (close = first). Every senior on a team is a co-captain. How crazy is that? How sad. False achievement is now rampant and is intended to promote "success." But instead, all this meddling by a well-intended system has created mediocrity.

And all this fake "success" is now creating the *opposite* of what was intended by the system. By not allowing that moment in time—that epiphany—when the perfectly capable C student realizes that the education system does not present the optimum goal for him or her, the system likely deprives the average student of the timing to seize the opportunity to "get it." By artificially frosting over that point in time, we firmly imprint "mediocre" on that kid's forehead instead of setting him or her free. That moment of realization is needed to set free the next small business creator in America.

But instead we steal that moment and falsify it with some fake grade to keep promoting some false dream the system itself created. We refuse to allow greatness in another direction to happen anymore. We force good grades on average students whether they want them or even earn them! And the most frustrating part of this absurd process is there is nothing wrong with being a C student. Nothing. Yet we dwell on it. We pretend everyone is an A student in something...aren't they?!

So by attempting to promote a better society, America's education system instead condemns more and more teenagers to mediocrity. And worse, kids are unable to break free. And worst of all, they think they are actually honor roll students! Instead of using school for what it is...using the cumulative effort of education to help mold a keen mindset for another direction...the system frustrates that natural progression for C students. Instead the system swallows the non-A student into what *the system* says is important. And in that horrific system where everyone is an A student in something, most are doomed to mediocrity.

Don't let it happen to you.

CHAPTER 2:

TEACHERS ARE GOOD PEOPLE
AND SCHOOL IS A GOOD PLACE

This chapter is what I refer to as the necessary disclaimer chapter. The place where an author must state what he or she is not saying, so that critics of a particular point of view cannot say something was implied by a particular statement, passage, or entire work. So please bear with this section.

The intent of this book is not to say that school is bad or that educators are not good people or don't intend to do great things with every student they encounter. Nothing is further from the truth. Almost without exception, educators that I have met are passionate about what they do, and the sacrifices they make every day to be teachers and stay in the education industry are extraordinary. Indeed, many lives—millions of lives—are changed for the better every day because of the teachers in America's schools.

These are deeply dedicated people who should not take this book in a negative way. Rather, I wish to have educators, parents, and students look upon the status of a C student in a different light: not as a young person who needs to somehow work harder, learn differently, or be tested differently so that he or she achieves some type of different type of intelligence or way of learning or above average grades. Rather, it may be even better if some C students don't actually pursue a better grade point average. It just might be plausible that they are fine with their current grade point average and that their lives may soon surpass every possible expectation of the wildest dreams of most honor roll students if these C students are allowed to develop along a different path.

It is also not the intent of this book to cast all C students in the same light. Not all C students should pursue the direction I espouse here. Indeed, many middle-of-the-road students are in fact better students that for whatever reason either chose not to pursue greater achievement (possibly laziness or poor study skills) or simply are not able. I am not stating that C students should give up a dream of their own if in fact it is a dream they actively pursue for themselves. What I am suggesting is that the honor roll is not the only dream to be pursued within the academic side of school. In fact, most kids are never told why they are even in school!

And that is the essence of this book: most parents and educators tend to lull kids into the process of pursuing good grades. I have been told by teachers to drop my child out of a higher-level course because he would have a greater prospect of achieving an A. As a result, kids are stuck in a process that appears to have no end and no purpose except for endless amounts of information being memorized or absorbed. We never actually tell them we are giving them the foundations and tools to develop rational thought, to think through a process or problem logically, creating the ability to identify problems and develop solutions. To the extent we tell kids at a younger age that rational thought is what they are pursuing then those students who are candidates for the non-honor roll path I am advocating will flush themselves out. They will be able to stand tall and identify themselves as free of the burden of the singular pursuit of the masses—the almighty A. They will be able to use the education system to sharpen their own logic and problem-solving skills. They will be encouraged from within to strive and work hard—for self-improvement, not grades. They will stop chasing good grades and start chasing their own dreams, using the system to help get them there.

What I am also not saying is that a vocational school direction is bad. Many public high school systems now offer alternative schools where a more vocational direction is desired. These programs are, in my view, training programs that should create excellent employees. The vocational direction in public education is an excellent addition and should not be discounted for many kids.

And finally the intent of this book is not to degrade the honor roll students and the parents who are proud of those students. I was an honor roll student and valedictorian of my high school class, an academic free ride at a top university. And many kids are good at school. It is their element. And they should fully enjoy their moment in the sun. Again, we desperately need heart surgeons and rocket scientists (although I am neither!). We can never have enough really smart people making our lives safer and better. And the top schools seek these kids out and reward this activity, as well they should. We have a better world because we have smart people and a system that rewards those people for being smart. But it is also okay not to be that good in school. After all, America is built by many, many, MANY more successful small business people who were not in the top ten or even twenty or thirty percent of their class.

So please...if you are a really smart person or an educator, *please* do not take this book as insulting. Aristotle said, "The sign of an enlightened person is the person who can entertain an opposing thought without accepting it." All I ask is that you consider the proposal put forth here—that all kids need not go through the neck of the hourglass. Rather, the path to great achievement may be through owning fifty car washes or figuring out the best way to get king crab legs from Alaska to New York City and Paris. And a 3.5 grade point average is not required for either of these scenarios. In fact, the system delivering the 3.5 may have actually discouraged the 3.5 GPA kid from taking the chance to *even think about starting* that king crab leg business.

CHAPTER 3:

THE AMERICAN SCHOOL SYSTEM

It's an Elementary Problem

To build anything that lasts a long time, you must build a solid foundation. In school years gone by, that foundation was found in spelling bees, teaching and understanding proper grammar, and memorization of poetry and multiplication tables. But no more. Calculators and creative spelling are now the norm. The best middle school math teacher I ever met recently told me that if he gave an exam on fractions to his top eighth-grade algebra class, that one-third of them would fail the exam. Not get a B or a C. Fail. That is a very sad statement.

And it's a sad statement because it is probably true. And the battle to understand fractions was lost well before that outstanding teacher stood in front of those eighth graders. It was lost in the beginning—in elementary school. Our system today has given in to the sound bite era. It believes we learn "better" not by memorization or drill, but by touching a subject lightly, moving on, and then seeing it again and again and again. We therefore create almost a distracted way of educating our kids. Just when they start to understand something the system moves on. Or the system allows an error to eventually correct itself—like spelling. Of course, the system does not have any remedies if a weakness does not correct itself.

So from the beginning, through our modern "standards-based" way of teaching, we deprive some of our kids the chance for success away from school. Right from the start, we refuse to teach little minds the benefits of hard work through really, *really* understanding the fundamentals. Some call it core knowledge. Opponents call it unnecessary drilling of disconnected facts. Whatever you call it, the system now discourages the process of building a strong foundation of fundamentals and instead wishes to give our kids "critical thinking skills." But don't kids have to first develop a knowledge base in order to then critically think? Don't they have to learn words before they can write a sentence? How do they develop creative writing without the basic tools to write creatively? Their little brains need to go through the difficulty of that foundation-building process so they can re-use that process later in life. And we are failing them miserably.

So our kids float through elementary school learning a little about a lot over and over—*hoping* they get it. And *hope is not a strategy* (Rick Page). Test scores in the early grades reward this survey style of education.

Tests seek to identify some knowledge early in many sides of a subject, so introducing a second grader to crude geometry or algebra such that they can answer a rudimentary question on the subject is regarded as superlative work. But sadly, an education based upon "a little about a lot" begins to fall down as the process later gets a little tougher. The kids simply don't have strong fundamentals, so they eventually fall down.

From a scientific perspective, I am told by some really smart people that repetition, memorization, and other such "drill" tasks actually help develop, strengthen, and extend neural pathways in the brain. And these neural pathways are multi-purpose and can themselves be linked. But that's for another book!

Middle School: How Our Schools Have Lied to America

An educator recently repeated something to me that gave me a chill: "It is not the job of a middle school to prepare kids for high school. It is the job of a high school to pick the kids up where a middle school leaves them."

Having researched the middle school movement, I believe this quote sums up the disaster of the American education system today in grades six through eight.

The kids come into middle schools knowing a little about more subjects by the time they reach the sixth grade than we ever did thirty or forty years ago. I didn't even know what the word "algebra" meant in the sixth grade. But today most kids in the sixth grade can do a very simple algebra problem. That's amazing, isn't it? Not if they can't multiply 7 x 8 in their heads, it's not. The kids come into middle school with an education that's a mile wide and an inch deep. I think someone once referred to it as a puddle education: smooth on the surface but not deep enough to sustain very much life.

And then the island mindset of a middle school education sets in: middle school is a rest stop, a place where adolescents go to be themselves and grow at their own pace. Academic preparation is no longer a priority. Everything is hard in life, so let's take these three years and take some pressure off. Let's just allow them to morph into adults during these fragile years. And let's place social/emotional needs above all others. Everyone will be an honor roll student for three years. Then we'll come back to reality and it's the high school's problem to take it from there.

We are losing the education battle in this country because we are abandoning our very own system. One hundred years ago, not many kids went to high school. Most had to drop out of school and work to support their families. So naturally it was the burden of the system to teach the basics to everyone before they left. And lo and behold something extraordinary happened. These kids with fundamentals in their education built

America. Not IBM or American Airlines, but Main Street America, where most jobs are created. Where we spend most of our time day-to-day. These kids that left before high school to work to support their families knew how to multiply, knew fractions, and how to write in compete sentences.

But not anymore. For some reason, the education system deems fundamentals to be less necessary. Progressive educational theories somehow deem emphasizing fundamentals as stifling creativity. In his book *What Does It Mean To Be Well Educated?*, Alfie Kohn actually brags about his wife achieving advanced degrees in medicine without an ability to spell or write correctly. Kohn suggests such disciplines would have taken away from her stratospheric rise. I guess Picasso didn't study basic art disciplines before he literally turned the art world on its ear. Of course he received classical training. Did he then become a classical artist for his entire lifetime? Did his classical education stifle his creativity? Of course not. It gave him two critical qualities:

- He knew how to be creative with his talent because the basics were now ingrained in his being. He had a great foundation—where the lines were so he could draw outside of them.
- He reached the point where he knew the system was not for him. He rejected the status quo; he rejected classical ways of doing things.

Ahhh…the epiphany moment.

It was necessary for Picasso to initially understand classical art in order for him to reject the same. One came from the other. You don't just become a cutting-edge philosopher or artist or businessperson until you know what other philosophers or artists or business-men do or have discovered—and perhaps have done incorrectly or inefficiently or at least differently. But true creativity can't be developed by not first teach-ing fundamentals in elementary school, by refusing to acknowledge the middle school responsibility of pre-paring kids for high school, and by giving out inflated grades to give kids and their parents a false sense of success. Instead, when we do this, we deprive our children and this country of many chances of being truly great. And sadly, by the time these kids get to high school, it's often too late to teach fundamentals. And we now see the devastating results of this failed philosophy across the country.

Grades Are Overrated...Especially in High School

You don't know it yet, but the most successful kids in your high school class are going to be the kids who are getting Cs right now. Or what should be Cs. Unfor-tunately schools today are all too eager to artificially prop up grades, so let's say really low Bs or fake Bs.

And this may surprise you, but there is a fundamen-tal misunderstanding that really good grades always reflect being smart. They don't. Many times they simply show *who is really good at schoolwork*. These top students know *how* and *when* to study as much as knowing the content of a particular subject. They know *how* to take good notes and *how* to do make-up projects if they happen to get a bad test score; in other words, they know how to play the school game. They are good *at* school, but not necessarily on their way to success after school ends. And I know this because that was me. And the most successful, content, and happiest people in my high school class were in the middle of the pack.

Huh?

But how is it possible to go to Duke or Harvard without great grades? It's not. As a matter of fact, it's impossible unless Mom or Dad gives a school millions of dollars a year. But let the top grade getters go to the best schools. That's right; let the others go to the top schools. Don't worry about it. How many times have you heard, "Yeah, he's really smart, but he doesn't have any common sense."? It's because many of these really smart kids are lost after they leave school. Or rather, they are destined not to chart their own course but serve someone else's. They are lost in the bubble world of academics. Lost in their parents' notion of a world where certainty and the elimination of risk are the primary goals in life. They figured out early that in order to please adults—i.e. parents, teachers, superiors—that top grades were the way to go. So that becomes the psyche: please my superiors...get good grades. And nothing else matters. Sure, some of these

kids are "well rounded" with extra curricular activities, but who dictates that? Mom and Dad, and they
do so in order to please the superiors and build the
resume for college. And the wrong mindset is born,
the one of doing what you are told. Be a good kid. Pay
your bills. Be a good employee. And whatever you do,
don't take any risk.

Key Question #1:   Should I work hard to get good
                   grades?

Key Answer #1:   No. You should work hard to
                   achieve the goal of a mature,
                   logical mind, not good grades.

Explanation:

Going to a top undergraduate school is probably
a greater indicator of securing a good job than true
success. Don't misunderstand me: <u>You should abso-
lutely go to college</u>. Let me repeat: it is less likely you
can be successful if you don't go to college. Are there
examples of successful people who did not go to college? Sure there are. Like ninety-year-old people who
smoked every day of their lives: they are out there, but
they are rare.

But what I am saying is don't go crazy chasing the
honor roll if you're not already an honor roll student.
That's not to say it's okay to be lazy. It's not. It's just
the opposite: the enlightened C student must work

really hard to a) secure a solid foundation, b) develop reason and logic, and at the same time, c) avoid the risk-averse trap of the education system.

Rule #1: KNOW WHY YOU ARE DOING WHAT YOU ARE DOING

Why are you in school? Really. Have you ever asked yourself or anyone else why you go to school? Have you ever sat down and thought...what the heck does chemistry or an algebra word problem *really* have anything to do with real life? I'll never use it. It's crap. Why do I need to sit through this stuff *every* day? And do homework in this stuff?!

Well, I have the answer for you, but it's not easy to understand. Not that you can't understand it, but rather because you've never been taught to understand it. So here goes:

Life is an algebra word problem and success comes when you solve that algebra word problem. Well, actually life is a never-ending series of algebra word problems, and success comes from figuring them out over and over again.

Are you throwing up yet?

If not, then here's why: success in life is simply finding out what's missing. Solving for X. That's it. It's all about finding the answer...with partial information. Get it? School is simply there to teach you how to solve for X, and X is what is missing. It's missing in almost anything—beauty products, affordable housing, clean water, trash disposal. And there are clues out there to help someone solve for X—the rest of the equation (in education terms). So school, and doing the drills and practicing, is teaching you *how to think rationally*, how to solve problems, because the person who solves the problem the best way—easiest, cheapest, fastest, and friendliest—wins. Yes, it's that simple.

You see, it's about inspired thought. To many honor roll students, figuring out when Jenny's train passes Johnnie's train is about succeeding on that exam—there isn't a connection to the greater goal of education. But the inspired American C student senses something else. He or she sits in the back of the class and thinks...those two damn trains to Buffalo that left the station at different times at different speeds *cannot* be all there is. No way. I am NOT here to learn when trains pass each other at different speeds and starting times (especially on the way to Buffalo). This *cannot* be all there is. Bingo. Right on. Light bulb goes on. When you say that to yourself for the first time you are on your way to being successful.

So, my dear young friends, the answer to "What am I doing in school?" is you are NOT studying algebra in algebra class, and you are not learning how to balance chemistry equations in chemistry class. No, you are not. Not at all. You are being taught how to think. How to solve for X rationally. You are in school to strive to improve your mind to help you become a conscious, self-actualizing person. To be human, if you will. Not to regurgitate but instead to think for yourself in order to arrive at a conclusion about something...about anything...and reasonably seek to solve for the missing answer. THAT is why you are in school.

Yes, you need to know multiplication and division cold. Percentages and fractions cold. Write in complete sentences and use either with or and neither with nor. Yes, you must have a solid foundation of core knowledge. And if you don't have it now, go get it at one of the tutoring companies out there or the pretty, smart girl or handsome, smart boy down the street. And then if you can sit in the back of the class and spend that painful time listening to the teacher drone on about covalent bonds and ionization while translating that into how those concepts will better prepare you to understand where the demand is in what you truly love to do, well then, you will be on your way to becoming one of the most successful kids in your class...regardless of your chemistry grade.

Know why you are doing what you are doing. Remember that. And if you don't know, ask. And keep asking if you don't find the answer that feels right in your gut. A friend of mine that is a very successful businessperson taught me to understand why I was doing what I was doing. Problem is: I was forty. I just hope you are fifteen or sixteen reading this, because it is the epiphany that will change your life.

CHAPTER 4:

ARE THEY TRAINING YOU
OR EDUCATING YOU?

"Between stimulus and response, there is space. In that space is our power to choose our response. In our response lies our growth and freedom." Victor Frankl

College: "I'll never get into college!" Phooey. There is a college for everyone. But let's review: the reason you go to school is to learn how to think rationally and learn how to work through and solve problems. Those are the key skills to a successful and happy life. If you are an average student, don't try to set yourself up to go to a "good" school or a wannabe "good" school, which is setting yourself up to fall into place....into *someone else's place*. You want to use school to get what *you* want, *not* be a product of it or, worse, one of its cogs.

Sadly, over the last forty years or so, in order for the American education system to "educate the masses," we have done a terrible disservice to the American dream. There are three tragic mistakes that now bog down the education system:

1. The perception that high achievement in school is the primary path to success in life
2. The inability of the system to actually educate America's youth
3. The tendency of the system to train instead of educate

1. High achievement in school is not the only path to success in life—and may not even be the best path.

Yes, the statistics are overwhelming: those that have higher degrees have higher incomes. But as Robert Kiyosaki pointed out in *Rich Dad, Poor Dad,* a big degree and higher income do not necessarily mean success—maybe just greater burdens to carry, such as feeding the tax man, the bank...and your boss.

There are countless books for those not educated at the best schools, beginning with Mark McCormack's *What They Don't Teach You at Harvard Business School.* Why is the market for these books so large? One simple reason: most successful small business people that have started their own businesses did not go to top schools like Harvard's business school. Harvard graduates typically go on to run large enterprises—and we need them, because they employ lots of people. But there are only twenty thousand companies that have greater than five hundred employees in the entire country. And there are almost *thirty million* businesses with less than five hundred employees! These are the entrepreneurs in the American system; they *are* the American system, and they are typically from the middle of the pack in high school and college. And as they grow their businesses, to the extent they lack the proper technical business management skills themselves to continue that growth, they are savvy enough to go out and hire really smart people to help run their businesses and do the legal and accounting work for them.

Please don't misunderstand what I am saying. The top schools are fabulous places that generate top talent, and many, many entrepreneurs who go on to start and run great companies graduate from these great institutions. What I am saying is the vast majority of the American system—indeed, the fabric of the American economy—is made up of average academic achievers who then go on to over-achieve in business, the arts, or in whatever field they are passionate.

People that go to Harvard or other top schools will most likely be successful. But what if you don't go to Harvard? What if you're a C student in an average American high school? As incredible as it may seem, the American system is counting on your success to continue our way of life. That's right. Our country is all about the average kid that makes it big and starts a business and hires people. *That* is what makes America what it is, the backbone that makes this country strong: more small business *employers*.

2. The American education system no longer educates our children.

A twentieth-century philosopher, C.S. Lewis, made a startlingly simple observation in his speeches collected in a short work, *The Abolition of Man*: the education system no longer gives children and young adults the basic fundamentals to build rational, reasonable thought. To Lewis, rational thought is what it means to be human.

Instead the education system teaches platitudes... truisms...answers. So success in the education system is translated into regurgitating these truisms or taught answers rather than developing the ability to construct a rational argument on one's own. What are the kids striving for? An answer to a history test? Of course not. We no longer give our kids strong foundations and then teach them how to think. Instead the system teaches them *what* to think. Answers. That is awful. Because if a young person is not properly educated to develop his or her own thoughts, then he or she grows up reacting emotionally to issues rather than rationally thinking through a problem. "Health care is a right." Okay, where do rights come from? What is a just society? A just person? What is justice? If a person cannot develop a rational construct, then society is deprived of problem solvers and we produce polarized, emotional reactions. Not good.

3. The education system is really a training system.

So if C.S. Lewis is right, then the education system is a misnomer—it does not really educate at all. By the way, Lewis made his observation in England in the 1940s! Instead I believe the education system seeks to train. The "education" system trains you how to get good grades, with each subject spewing its own syllabus of information. For what? How is it helpful to know facts or truisms without the ability to think rationally about any particular issue at hand?

So in order to be successful in life—I mean truly successful—why would you expend your effort getting trained really well in order to think and act the same way other people do? Answer: you wouldn't. But that's what the smart kids do. The straight A student is rewarded by regurgitating what his or her teachers say. Ring the bell...get some cheese...Billy's bus overtakes Jenny's in ninety minutes after they leave Buffalo...and the A grades flow. I am not saying that it is not necessary to build a solid foundation of knowledge and problem solving skills. Just the opposite. We need to do that. We must first build strong foundations. But first, build a strong foundation of fundamentals then on top of that foundation develop rational thought. And most of the time, the system never acknowledges this goal of rational, logical thought.

Every once in a while, there is a glimmer of hope as some members of the education system seem to indicate a vague awareness of the problem they are creating. Take the case of graduate business programs featured in the *New York Times* on January 10, 2010, especially the University of Toronto. "MBA" stands for master in business administration. In the *Times* article, the people running the top MBA programs seem to indicate that they are now just realizing that decision making may be a good characteristic in their graduates. Wow. That a liberal arts education may have some merit in developing a rational, keen mind in the real world of business. This is news? That training isn't the end all?

But the true tragedy of this eureka moment within the education system is the response, which basically says let's incorporate decision-making *training* into an MBA program. This response is wrong on so many levels. What if a liberal arts major wants an MBA? Should he avoid the now trendy liberal arts MBA programs? Can a graduate business program do a good job of delivering a condensed version of a liberal arts education to poorly educated but highly trained students? What does this liberal arts effort say about the education system below the graduate degree level? Once again, the system approaches an education problem backwards by reacting instead of being pro-active. Instead of the University of Toronto or any other trendsetting school demanding that its business school applicants have at least a reasonable level of undergraduate classes such as philosophy and other liberal arts pursuits, it waters down its own precious two years of time by trying to make up for the apparent deficiency in its applicants. Undergraduate programs now do this with remedial math and language arts programs to make up for weak high school programs. What's next? Medical schools offering undergrad biology and organic chemistry?

Development of a keen, decisive mind takes a long time. There are no short cuts. Logic, reason, or "critical thinking" in edu-speak, is built upon a solid foundation. It cannot be condensed into a semester or two of training—whether you are twelve or twenty-four. What the head of the University of Toronto is attempting to do is band-aid a systemic problem. The underlying system should be developing his applicants' decisive minds through twelve to sixteen years of education.

Thus developing critical thinking skills, like success in life, is not a race and not everyone passes the same mile-markers at the same age. Take your time and insist on getting it right—and if you sense weakness in your foundation, then go back and repair it. Colonel Sanders was sixty-five years old and showed his plan to hundreds of people before he was successful franchising his Kentucky Fried Chicken business. Many times, great things take time to develop (see Malcolm Gladwell's ten thousand hours in *Outliers*).

CHAPTER 5:

THE FEARED BELL CURVE

"By three methods we may learn wisdom: First by reflection, which is the noblest; second, by imitation, which is the easiest; and third, by experience, which is the bitterest." Confucius

Charles Murray and Richard Herrnstein wrote an excellent book entitled *The Bell Curve*. And while factually correct, I believe Murray's approach, especially in a subsequent book, *Real Education,* misses a fantastic opportunity. Rather than point to the fact that the majority is in the middle (say, the middle sixty percent), the author props up the old argument that we should view the world in a fifty-fifty perspective: a top half and a bottom half. His basic belief is that the world is run by people in the top half (or top ten or twenty percent)—the smarter percentage of the population. He is probably right considering that large corporations and governments run the world. But what makes America *great* is not GM or Exxon or the federal government. What makes America *great* is what C students do: start and run small businesses. Almost thirty million of them.

In simple terms, a bell curve is a bending line shaped like a bell (hence the name), and it represents a natural distribution of just about anything. How fast we run. How tall we are. How fat cats get. How well we achieve in school. A bell curve plots data along a line from the worst to the best (or shortest to tallest, or slowest to fastest, etc.). And typically in a natural distribution, the largest numbers in a sample fall somewhere toward the middle—about *average*.

I heard that someone recently wrote that the problem with a bell curve is that it automatically sentences half of us to below average, which is why so many people dislike it! (I could not find the quote, so my apologies for no credit.) But there's that top/bottom perception again.

It's actually a pretty funny line. And it's true. Half of us *are* below average in pretty much everything. Above average in some things but below average in a bunch of things too. We don't really like to think in those terms because it doesn't really feel that good. But why is a "top half/bottom half" perspective the right way to view this curve—or the world? I would argue it is not.

Here is an example of a bell curve:

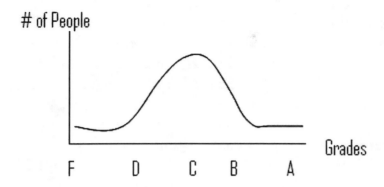

So a bell curve is just a scientific way to visually or graphically demonstrate or explain a distribution of something. The speed of field mice or the size of the American garage. There are some really slow mice, a few really fast mice, but most mice run at about the same speed—average. The same for the size of garages: a few are really small or really big, but most are the same size—average. So by counting along a graph for almost anything that is measurable in nature, as one moves along a horizontal axis, the closer to zero, the lower on the curve; then the curve rises until it reaches the average/mean/median, then falls again toward the floor as fewer and fewer achieve the high end of the range.

So in this visual display of a natural distribution, 1) if we want to discuss *half* of the population, should we look at a top, bottom, or middle half? And 2) why is it that everyone wants to be above average?

Here's a way to look at a bell curve you may have never heard before: look at a bell curve as a wave in the ocean or a mountain at sunrise. As a surfer, how good is your ride if you are way out front—at the bottom (right) of the wave? That's not a ride, that's getting wet! Instead, the best ride is being on top of the curve...on top of the wave...paddling in a controlled, consistent, purposeful manner. Gaining an ever so slight advantage and letting the wave carry you forward. If you try too hard or start too early, then you wind up too far out in front of the wave struggling, working on your own instead of using the strength of the wave behind you.

The same concept applies to a hiker wanting to be at the top of a mountain to see the sunrise. It is the *wise* hiker that knows it is best to be on top or just barely over the top. The overly eager early starter climbs right over the peak too early—and misses the beauty of the sunrise altogether. This concept is a key to success, meaning understanding that being on top of the curve is not being average but rather is a vantage point to see what others at the bottom of the curve do not see. Being on top of the curve allows for failure, an ability to truly learn, and to gain wisdom. It is not enough to be smart to be successful in life. One must be wise. And wisdom comes from failure. Sometimes several failures. Without fear of failure.

So let's use the bell curve to map how smart people are. A few people are not very smart. Most people are about average, and just a few people are really, really smart.

The education system hates the bell curve. Yet it tells the truth: most kids are of average intelligence. That fifty percent in the middle. Not the top. Not the bottom. Middle. What's the matter with that? Well, it means someone is going to fail or have his or her feelings hurt. But as we all know, someone is going to fail, bell curve or not.

And educators hate that. Why should someone have to fail...or be in the middle of the pack? Why can't everyone be an A or B student? If someone gets Cs and Ds, it might hurt someone's self-esteem or otherwise discourage him or her, won't it? So we cannot take that chance. So what do schools do? They come up with a system so everyone can succeed. And success means....good grades. Not that the grades reflect that anything has actually been learned. Instead grades become relative to that student's perceived progress.

But again, what's the matter with occasionally failing or being average? As we know, it's not the failing that's important. The key is—rather, the *American* key is—who gets back up, brushes himself or herself off, and says, "that hurts and I'm not going to do that again"...and jumps back into the game. That's the key to failure and learning. And the *wiser* person will learn not to fear this process.

I didn't say *smarter.* I said *wiser.*

This reality check is a critical break-through point for success. Thomas J. Stanley documents this fact in his outstanding book *The Millionaire Mind* in which he surveys millionaires and describes their make-up. He cites an almost universally common event in successful people's early lives: "During (the surveyed millionaires') formative years, some authority figure such as a teacher, parent, guidance counselor, employer, or aptitude testing organization told them: *you are not intellectually gifted.*" Did that hurt? Probably. What are you going to do about it? How about go be great at something other than school? Don't quit, but use school to get what *you* want, not what the system wants to sell.

Key Question #2: Where does wisdom come from in real life?

Key Answer #2: It comes from failure...and starting over again. Or, as Confucius says in the quote at the beginning of this chapter, it comes from experience (which is the bitterest method of acquiring wisdom).

That's right...failure and starting over. And a big problem with our public education system is that it is built so that no one fails (or very, very few people do), so no one has to start over. Educators instead choose the second choice—imitation. In other words, we are not allowing kids to truly gain experience in order to gain wisdom. Instead the education system attempts to take the easiest way out—according to Confucius—by allowing and indeed *encouraging* imitation. By simply teaching truisms, answers, and regurgitation of what is taught, our system attempts to convey wisdom. As a result, we generate trained people that lack wisdom useful in the real world and therefore lack the ability to truly achieve in life.

Key Question #3: What dooms people to certain mediocrity?

Key Answer #3: Fear of failure.

And because of this fear of failure or avoidance of experience that generates true wisdom, we have built an education system with a bell curve that looks like this:

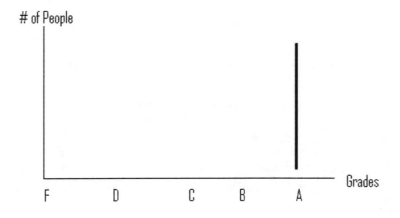

The goal of the education system is have everyone become an honor roll student. But true honor roll students have been that way almost from birth. They have always been near the top. Early readers, overzealous parents...whatever the reason. But sadly, the one tragic mistake they learn is: don't take chances. I'll talk about more of this risk-averse issue later in the book, but for now I'll call this tragedy a fear of failure. Because for honor roll students, to not make a good grade, to not make the honor roll, well, it's the kiss of death. Why? Well, then I won't be able to go to a good college, that's why. Well then, let me ask you a question: is there a *bad* college or university?

Here are some successful people that I admire:

Richard Branson – Because Branson is British, I can't comment on their education system; I just know he's very cool and has been very successful in music, airlines, etc.

Frank Perdue (deceased) – Food; chicken

Don Imus (almost deceased) – Radio talk show

Jake Burton Carpenter – Snowboards, clothing

From what I have learned about these people, my general understanding is that they were average students in school. They were probably kids that watched the A students from the back of the classroom. They probably realized that a classroom wasn't their best environment. So they went out and found the environment they *would* be good in...and became more successful than all their classmates combined. And in the examples I reference, these people appear to me to be not only financially successful but are (or were in their lives) genuinely happy to boot.

CHAPTER 6:

WHY SCHOOLS GIVE FAKE As AND Bs: THE SELF-ESTEEM GAME AND WHY MANY EDUCATORS HAVE IT BACKWARDS

Many, many educators believe—incorrectly—that if a kid has high self-esteem, then that kid will achieve academically. So educators over the last several decades have embraced twisted notions like "multiple intelligences" and other theories to support this utopian belief: that everyone is an A student in something. And if those students just received As and Bs and made the honor roll (hooray....hooray...hooray), then something magical would happen. Those kids who previously thought they were dumb and had low self-esteem would then start to achieve because their self-esteem had been magically propped up.

And that is deadly wrong.

Deadly wrong because this practice of giving away As and Bs beginning in the middle school years and making everyone an honor roll student a) masks the problem of a weak foundation and b) deprives the future successful C student the right to go through the process of realizing that what most people are chasing is wrong for them, and that success for them is going to come from another direction. Instead these future entrepreneurs are lulled to sleep with an easy A—not challenged, but rather promoted, with the system avoiding low grades at all costs for fear of further lowering self-esteem. So instead of telling me I am just not going to make it as a figure skater, they give me trophies, tell me I'm most improved, and award me first place in the costume category. But I'm a lousy skater. I'm not going to the Olympics and have Dick Button call my name. Please tell me this so I can take my career in a different direction.

When my second son was six or seven, our town's coach-pitch baseball league rule was no one struck out. Swing until you get a hit. And one kid just could not. The coach crept closer and closer. Nothing. The little boy began to cry. The coach kept lobbing as the boy's little shoulders shook. It would not end; it seemed like almost fifty pitches. The no-failure rule created the worst failure of all: crushing that little boy's true self-esteem.

So the system not only supports itself by convincing everyone that making the honor roll will solve all ills, but that if you just had a little more self-confidence, you too would join the "A" club. And to help a student get there, the system pays the first few years of club membership dues for free: just for showing up, you'll get As and Bs. Then you too will see that all is well with the world, that you too are an honor roll student. Don't you feel good about the future? Don't you feel successful? Gimme a break.

In reality, true self-esteem comes from actual achievement, not the other way around. Kids are not dumb. We cannot tell someone she is a good soccer player or good violin player. And we cannot tell someone he is a good math student. They hear another kid—once—and they know. And it's not a bad thing. The system is so worried about low self-esteem, so afraid of failure, so afraid of *risk*, that no one should be subject to that—when, in fact, the opposite is true. Adults handling failure of a child maturely is the way—perhaps the only real way—a kid will learn how to succeed.

A person must feel the sting of failure in order to know how that feels and then not want that feeling anymore. By faking honor rolls, the system deprives our kids of the opportunity to right their own ships. Instead the system forces an artificial course for every child possible down this channel that feeds the education industry: achievement equals As and Bs whether there is anything behind those grades or not. So instead of our top entrepreneurial C students figuring out that school work is not their thing, not the direction they should try to excel in, these future business starters, job creators, and problem solvers are led to the slaughter. They are forced into the apex of the education system with truly gifted students, and then the real failure comes with a loud thump all at once—often times devastating. The real C student is never allowed to realize early enough how weak his or her foundation is or correct it. Lost forever is the individual who could have had an opportunity to truly learn early in his or her education, who sees the train wreck ahead, and could have stepped off the tracks.

This awareness is often referred to as self-knowledge—a recognition of weaknesses in an honest manner and an admirable quality indeed.

Another Reason Why the System Promotes Good Grades: Money

Let's face it: there is a lot at stake in the education business. Imagine what would happen to "top" schools, "top" educators, etc. if parents and children came into school not really caring about grades. What would happen if most people (because most people are C students) rejected the notion that "everyone is an A student in something" and instead stated: just give me the fundamentals and teach me how to think and solve problems. You can keep the grades.

Really…what would happen? Lots of people would lose their jobs and lots of money would be lost. Because if people really understood that the current system was actually hurting our brightest students by teaching them to be risk averse in their quest for the perfect score AND hurting our future business-starting

C students by artificially propping them up as A students in something, then people would reject that system. In its stead, we would return to a basic liberal arts education instead of the training system we now have.

The problem is the system receives free money (taxes) every day to perpetuate what the system wants instead of what kids need. The system wants lots of jobs and high pay, benefits, retirement, etc. So we spend lots of money on better systems, the latest research-based techniques, and of course bigger and better buildings. We build bureaucracies to support the system, bureaucracies that are self-feeding, creating more jobs and more work. Regardless of the rhetoric of "student-centered education," the system is centered on itself, the educators and the supporting infrastructure.

Then the system creates envy. The elite colleges are those everyone strives to attend. That town has a better school system than the other town, etc. In essence, the education system sells the public on what *the system* is good at—not what the kids really need.

What if you were to go into your local high school and ask the principal to name the most successful people to come out of the school in the last twenty years? What do you think the principal would say off the top of his or her head? That's right. He or she would probably list the kids that went on to the top colleges. Because lots of educators view education in itself as success. Those kids bought what the high school was selling…and then bought some more of the "best" at an elite college.

Then ask that principal to name the people that own the top ten or twenty locally owned businesses in town. He or she may be able to name a couple of people, but will be hard pressed to remember many more of them at all—because they did not stand out in the education system's highly structured rewards system—surely an A student in *something*.

So there is a disconnect between what the education system sells and what people need. Sadly, I have heard it said that the American education system is as much a jobs program as it is an education program. And to protect itself, the system must not allow C students to pursue their own course of education. The system must reject the pursuit of rational thought for C students because it would greatly reduce the money flowing into the system. Instead it supplants true educational needs of our C students with vocational training, which of course requires more facilities, instructors, and of course more money. Get an A being trained to be an auto mechanic; when that high school should be encouraging a part-time job after school for the C student while keeping that kid in class, providing that C student a solid foundation and then developing logic and rational thought, so the C student can then go out and start his or her own business in the auto industry.

II.
Fixing The Problem:

What Students, Parents, Communities,
and our Schools should do to
Re-establish the Correct Mindset
for the American Dream…and
the American Economy

CHAPTER 7:

SO WHAT SHOULD WE DO?

"The task of a modern educator is not to cut down jungles, but rather to irrigate deserts." C.S. Lewis

Schools should begin openly and often to tell their students in the sixth, seventh, and eighth-grade years that the next seven years are going to be somewhat hard and confusing. And schools should let the kids know that it's going to be okay if some of the topics discussed are not fully absorbed by them. The students should keep the following in mind: school is about exercising one's mind, about developing logical reasoning. Not necessarily to memorize or regurgitate facts or answers, but to enable the mind to grow and develop its ability to rationally work through complex thoughts and dilemmas. This developing mind is what these students should strive to attain. Problems in life, whether they are personal or work related, require an ability to logically work through tough issues that are faced every day. Success in life comes from our ability to find solutions where they are not readily apparent.

That is the "constancy of purpose" that educators and school systems should keep at the forefront of your education. Above a solid foundation established in the first through eighth grade, it is not really about anything else other than gaining the tools of "how to think." And in order for your young mind to develop properly, it must venture into some difficult territory, addressing tough questions and challenges. The education system should not simplify things and eliminate difficult issues. Yet that's what the education system does all the time. It simply teaches a truism—a statement of opinion posed as a fact. The education system teaches the answer. Let's take an easy example:

"Racism is wrong."

From as early as the first grade, we are taught that racism is wrong. And of course, racism *is* wrong. But at what point does the education system give you the tools to understand why racism is wrong? Does a typical middle school and high school delve into what a just person does or how a just society arrives at its laws? How are you challenged to think through these dilemmas logically? Are you forced to reason through these issues? Or are you just asked to repeat these truisms? Do you get an A if you are able to cite examples of racism like the KKK or heroes like Martin Luther King Jr.?

Again, racism *is* wrong. But the system serves no one if the system does not take these issues and allows students' developing minds to explore these "jungles." Instead the system chooses to cut down that jungle and other jungles instead of "irrigating the desert" of the young mind. It's dangerous in a jungle. Many things can harm you and even eat you. But if the experience of surviving the jungle trail and coming out the other side safely is taken away from us, then aren't we deprived in many ways? And if the system avoids these relatively easy jungles to negotiate early in the process, then how are young developing minds supposed to navigate tougher jungles once they are on their own? In short, the system takes a short-term solution and creates a long-term problem for society by teaching truisms and platitudes rather than giving its students the tools to work through these issues on their own.

So there it is again. Logical thought. Reason. Problem solving. The whole purpose of being in school. To develop a reasonable mind. To be able to work through life's challenges on your own in a *risky* environment through a reasoned process. Not regurgitating a fact or a true statement here or there. But to reason through something and come out the other side in a better place. And hopefully make the world around you a safer and better place in the process.

CHAPTER 8:

FOUNDATION AND FUNDAMENTALS

Okay, so if you've read this far and not burned this book, then you might be interested in a subject-by-subject perspective on what I believe you should be getting out of education. Sick of hearing me talk about it, my teenage daughter recently asked me why no one in school ever told the kids why they were in school. Hmmm. Good question. Well, I am trying to answer that question throughout this book.

In *Cultural Literacy*, E.D. Hirsch attempts to identify specific topics, facts, etc. each person should master in school. While noble in its intent to maintain our current western civilization orientation, it swims against the progressive movement that has perhaps permanently seized the higher ground when it comes to subject content. Therefore the outcome we should be focused on is the macro result of a public K-12 education and not just content.

So to counter the specificity of an E.D. Hirsch and his *Cultural Literacy* as well as the vagueness of today's progressive non-judgmental learn-when-you-feel-like-it agenda, this chapter tries to answer the basic question: what should you get out of each subject area?

Are you ready? Here goes:

K-8:

Language Arts: Spelling, vocabulary, and grammar at a true grade level. Effective verbal communication in life after school is critical to personal and professional success. Solid verbal communication skills, in fact, determine how someone views the world. I think Charles Murray said something like this in *Real Education,* and I agree. The ability to listen, speak, read, and especially write well are priceless. And those K-8 skills above all others will improve your chances of success.

Math: Addition, subtraction, multiplication, division, fractions, and decimals—by heart.

Note: If you are fourteen or fifteen and do not have these K-8 skills, then go get them. It will take guts to admit the use of a calculator more than necessary. Or the need to use the green squiggly line in Microsoft Word to identify grammatical errors. But if you are honest with yourself, it's not too late. *Every* middle school and high school teacher would be honored to help you catch up. If you ask, then you will receive the help. Go get it. Those skills are critical for your success for the rest of your life.

High School:

By the eighth grade, you should have your solid foundation in reading, writing, and math. Again, this is critical, and if you don't have them, go back and get them. You'll be glad you did.

High school, in my opinion, is where you begin the macro quest of logical, rational thought. Problem solving. Many school systems and educators attempt to start "critical thinking" skills before ninth grade. I believe this is a mistake. A student cannot critically think without basic skills and core content. But tell the kids *why* they are learning those building blocks. Then, after the eighth grade, the focus should shift. Yes, you should still learn skills and content, and lots of it. But the overarching priority for you should be an expanding ability to think rationally, to develop an enlightened mind. And this context should be openly communicated—often.

MATH:

Algebra:

You should be learning that solving for X is what life is all about. The manipulation of equations (multiply both sides by 4 to eliminate the fraction, blah, blah, blah) does three things:

1. <u>Exercise</u>: It exercises your brain to think logically and to anticipate the next step (recognition of patterns from partial information). Initially that may be by trial and error. But through the discipline of exercises similar but slightly more challenging than the previous one, your brain will build muscle mass—well, sort of. It will be able to work longer and harder. It will become less intimidated by slightly harder problems. Exercise progress is slow and methodical because it takes time to build beautiful muscles—arms, legs, or brain—well, sort of.

2. <u>Logic and Balance:</u> Algebra teaches you that if you multiply by 4 on one side, you have to do the same on the other side. Imbalance is bad karma. Ying and yang and all that. Logical sequence is good. It leads you to the right conclusion: a result. A right answer. A decision.

3. <u>Life *is* solving for X</u>. Finally, you should translate those hated word problems into conversations about everyday life. If I make $2,000 per month after I graduate from college, but only $1,250 per month if I don't go to college, then how much better off am I if I go to college until the age of twenty-two instead of working? Am I better off at forty? At sixty? Solve for X

whether you are counting change in your pocket to buy a newspaper or figuring out if people will buy the new caffeine-laced milk drink you want to sell. Solve for X....solve for X...solve for X...it is what people do every day in almost every endeavor undertaken on a successful path. Algebra might be the most important core skill class you will ever take to help you establish a base of logic and problem solving ability.

Geometry:

Recently I heard a radio interview with the comedienne Paula Poundstone. The topic turned to being a parent, and she told a story where her daughter had been asked by a teacher to come up with three real life uses of bisecting an angle. She said she could only think of cutting the last piece of pizza or cake between two hungry kids. In other words, there aren't many real life uses for bisecting an angle—or for most of what you learn beyond the K-8 skills discussed above. So are they a waste of time? No. Are there specific geometric tasks for most of us in real life? Probably not many. But how about the mind's development of logic and reasoning? Huge reason to struggle through geometry. Huge.

1. Exercise: Your brain gets bigger (not really, but a symbolic thought) and better if you exercise it. Just like your arm or leg muscles. Geometry is a great exerciser, and the graphics of geometry

really help crystallize fundamental logic and reason in a visual way.

2. <u>Logic:</u> Proofs. The geometry proof. Wow. Are those a pain in the neck or what?! And like most kids, you will struggle with them and probably hate them. And that's okay. But they will teach your brain to think logically, sequentially, and rationally. And that is what you need to get out of the exercise of geometry. Sure, if you go into engineering, then geometry and physics will be really important. But for now, muscle through it and understand that it is really teaching you logical sequence, and be okay with just that.

Calculus:

1. <u>Exercise and Logic:</u> See above.

2. <u>Dealing with Irregularity in the World</u>: I am going to contradict myself here: For the most part, solving for X is not perfect. In fact, almost everything around you is not a perfect arc or circle or square. Calculus is a tool helping in the art and science of recognizing that fact. It should teach you that if you divide a really complicated problem into smaller bite sizes, then you can conquer anything. As the old saying goes, you eat an elephant one bite at a time. So that area under the squiggly line? As

X approaches infinity...blah, blah, blah. You can't count to infinity. But you can understand that irregularity can be broken down into smaller understandable pieces. There. That's calculus.

I said I was going to contradict myself. That's because an underlying theme of this book is that for every action there is an equal and opposite reaction. The world—and success in this world—relies on balance, and acknowledging the fact that the world is pretty much perfect (not our lives, but the world in and of itself is nearly perfect in almost every way). "For every action there is a reaction." Isaac Newton. The guy discovered gravity *and* invented calculus. Genius. I mean the concept/statement about action and reaction, not the man.

I am sure he was a genius, but I love the statement because it is so simple to understand. I'll probably say it a lot in this book, but I think someone else said "genius is in simplicity." Like $E = mc^2$. Not sure I could tell you why it's that simple, but it is genius that Einstein reduced the relationship between energy, mass, and the speed of light into a saying/equation every third grader can repeat. Genius is in simplicity. And a measure of your success in life will be your ability to simplify what you do. Remember that. Simple is better than complex in almost everything. And a great way to simplify things is to break complex, irregular issues into bite-size pieces—just as calculus teaches us.

SCIENCE:

Earth Science:

Understand the environment from the perspective that almost everything you do from here on out will have a cost associated with it relative to the environment. There will be taxes and fees put on everything that pollutes. And that spells opportunity. Understand how the natural world works, from ground water to volcanoes to rare earth elements to wind and weather. The next one hundred years will focus on Mother Earth and protecting it. Be a part of that effort and be successful.

Biology:

Organisms on earth are pretty much perfect. Biology will teach you symmetry and the food chain. Why do we have two lungs? Two ears and eyes, a left and a right side? Same with a lion, a grasshopper, and most fish. Why have sharks been around since before the dinosaurs and why does a cell membrane let sodium in and potassium out? Because there must be balance in the world or it gets angry and creates balance. If there are too many male frogs, they mutate and change to females to maintain population growth. (Can you imagine waking up the opposite sex than when you went to sleep?! Now that's Mother Nature getting a little upset about balance!)

Seriously, biology teaches us about the beauty of living organisms in this perfect world of ours. How do animals (including humans) behave instinctively when they are hungry, raising their young, or are cornered? Biology is about perfect function and going with the flow to maximize survival chances. Swim upstream and perish from exhaustion. We must see human existence for what it is and see the opportunity in that existence. We are bound to spend money on the basic items that we deem essential to our biological presence on earth: food, shelter, and clothing. And the art of success in this world is either supplying a better form or variation of one of those essentials—or convincing people that what you are selling should be valued sufficiently so they should turn over their hard-earned dollars to you in exchange for whatever you are selling.

Chemistry:

Chemistry is about balancing equations—because life is generally in balance. Chemistry *is* life. It does not exist unless one can balance the equation or, rather, it exists in a volatile state until the equation is balanced. And existing in a volatile state is not good. So chemistry teaches us that nature seeks balance. And we should therefore do the same in life as well as seek opportunities where short-term imbalance opportunities exist.

If, however, we view chemistry as simply another science that we don't understand and that we'll never need to know how sulfuric acid is created, then our chemistry classes have failed to improve our lives. Don't lose perspective. Take from your chemistry classes what you need, not what someone tells you is important.

Physics:

What goes up must come down.

For every action, there is an equal and opposite reaction.

Objects in motion tend to stay in motion.

Friction slows things down.

I can assure you that almost all of the time these physics statements are true in *so* many other things in life...especially in our economy. When things run smoothly and are managed well, business tends to be better. But when things are interrupted—if "friction" is introduced—then things tend to go badly, meaning they slow down. And most of the time, maintaining a healthy speed (i.e. staying in motion) is important for success in almost all things.

And again, don't all these thoughts sound reasonable, even logical? Of course they do. So physics is again developing your growing brain to think in logical lines—a straight and clear path from A to B. (How do I get there? How do I solve for X?)

SOCIAL STUDIES:

History teaches us a) don't repeat bad choices made by other people, b) copy good ideas and make them better, c) the world is a very big and very small place at the same time, and d) big impacts in the world really do come from a few courageous individuals. See the world for what it is and be one of those individuals. Remember, high school grades don't have much to do with it.

LANGUAGE ARTS:

In order to be successful, someone must be able to communicate ideas *clearly* to someone else, especially in small groups, especially in order for that someone else to pull out his or her wallet and pay for whatever it is you are selling. This communication takes many forms. In business, it may take the form of presentations, brochures, advertising, letters, speeches, team meetings, and simple sales calls. Again, logic and reason come into play, and if someone uses an illogical reason for not buying your product or service, you must be able to recognize the lack of logic quickly and be able to clearly describe a solution—in a very nice way, of course!

Poetry:

Poetry teaches us rhythm, passion, heartache, and love. Success in life requires rhythm and passion (and always involves heartache, and if you are lucky, love). There is a steadiness to success, and things like music, poetry, and other timing activities allow the brain to sense the broad, steady rhythm in life. Successful people swim with the flow, if you will. Unsuccessful people swim against the tide. They don't understand the rhythm of life's waves. They just see and hear crash, crash, crash! And the struggle goes on...

And passion! If someone can feel the passion in great poetry—when it goes to your soul—then you know what life should be about. The most successful people in the world are passionate about what they do. Most people misunderstand that and negatively describe passion as obsession. When you hear someone refer to someone else as obsessed with something, count on the speaker as probably swimming against the tide in his or her life—and is someone who probably hates poetry.

By the way, lots of poetry should be read out loud. When you hear Dylan Thomas's words out loud in the arrangement he chooses—or any other great poet—the words literally make you stop speaking. For me, they make me freeze my thoughts. I say to myself, wow, how does a writer even think of something like that, never mind write it down so concisely? Poetry just crystallizes life perfectly. It is not humanly possible to be any more concise. It cannot be said any better. That's what poetry does for me: simplifies complex thoughts and feelings in a concise, almost perfect rhythm while often displaying great passion. Capture how a poet feels about his or her subject and incorporate that into your mindset—good stuff.

Writing:

Unfortunately I cannot be broad or theoretical here. Writing is a skill necessary to communicate clearly. Master it and be successful, but be aware that it takes practice, practice, practice.

Know how to develop an essay:

- topic
- thesis sentence
- organize by major divisions
- topic sentence for each paragraph
- write paragraphs
- write intro paragraph
- write conclusion paragraph

Know the methods of expository writing:

- compare and contrast
- classification (take many and categorize)
- reasons and examples

- process analysis
- division – one object and divide into parts

SUMMARY

To beat a dead horse, so to speak, school is not about learning much of anything specific (except K-8 fundamentals). Yes, E.D. Hirsch makes a good point about his five thousand points of cultural literacy, but for the makers of the American dream, the local business creator, the person doing the hiring—*the C student*—school is about exercising that pea-sized brain we all start with in first grade.

We must become problem solvers, even problem identifiers. Yes, we must have the K-8 fundamentals. Problem identifying is *opportunity identifying*. And problem identifiers and solvers are the most successful in their personal and professional lives.

CHAPTER 9:

IS RISK GOOD OR BAD?

"It is always the adventurers who do great things, not the sovereigns of great empires." Charles DeMontesquieu

Practical definition of "bureaucracy": an environment where zero risk is taken and therefore no decision or progress is made.

Think about it: the only way you can be wrong is if you make a decision. Many will say, well, not making a decision is sometimes wrong. True, but that's rare to prove; you can always say you needed more time or more information, etc. Thus the art of being part of a bureaucracy is positioning yourself to never have to actually make a decision. Sounds crazy, doesn't it? But that's what bureaucratic systems create. A risk-free work environment. It's risky making a decision...hey, you might be wrong.

Schools are bureaucracies and breed a bureaucratic mindset even in their students. Here is a great teacher, Steve McKenzie from Dover, New Hampshire. He writes a column on education for the *Foster's Daily Democrat*, the local paper: "I never volunteer to be the scribe for any group of which I am a member. Know why? I can't stand to run the risk of misspelling a word. Do you have any idea how embarrassing it is to be an English teacher and misspell a word?"

In my experience interacting with educators, Mr. McKenzie's risk aversion is not unique within the education profession. Educators as a group tend to be risk avoiders. And who is trained to not take a risk? Bureaucrats...and really good students. Of course I'm generalizing, but think about the premise. Bankers tend to be A students. Same with lawyers and accountants. Doctors are A students. By definition, most accounting, legal, and medicinal work is performed to reduce or even eliminate risk—standardized systems, legal language to cover all possible scenarios, etc.

Mind you, bankers, doctors, lawyers, and accountants are not bad people. But they tend to be risk averse and support the American economic system rather than build it. Reasonable risk takers build a system, or a city, or an economy, or a country. I'm not talking about reckless people. I'm talking about people who see an opportunity where most others see risk. Some people only see risk. Others see only opportunity. These are considered crazy people because they cannot discern between reasonable risk and recklessness. And then there are risk assessors and reasonable risk takers.

And of course reasonableness is in the eye of the beholder. Some people see the horizon clearer than others. Sailing off to that horizon may be risky to many, yet not so risky to some. But there are those who don't even look at the horizon of opportunity and never step out of line for any reason. That's a mindset destined for mediocrity. Ironically, many overachievers in school become destined for mediocrity (like the author) *because of a learned avoidance of risk*. And mediocrity breeds safe places like bureaucracies—and this mindset is taught in school.

So is risk a bad thing? Are you a skier? Is a trail through the glades and moguls riskier than a beginner slope? Is that a bad thing? Not for you. But for someone who does not know what he or she is doing, risk is really bad. Was it risky for Apple to offer songs for sale on line for ninety-nine cents each and build the iPod around the notion that people would actually *pay* for songs when so many people were illegally downloading music for free on the Internet? How did that risky move work out for Apple? Was that bad for them? A couple of billion good reasons shows us all why taking that risk wasn't all so bad.

Such is the American dream—and the difference between A students and C students. Ask yourself this question: do the A students you know take a lot of risks? I'm not talking about stupid risks like driving fast, drugs, or alcohol. That is recklessness, not risk taking. I'm not talking about risking life and limb in a reckless manner. I'm talking about:

- seeing opportunity and understanding that some risk goes with that opportunity;

- assessing risk, studying it, and attempting to quantify it;

- embracing risk as part of an opportunity;

- managing risk on an ongoing basis.

Those steps are the key to success in America, and it is my belief and the overriding theme of this book that the American education system is depriving both the C student and the A student from embracing this model.

Here is a problem with our education system: it teaches our A students to avoid risk. Because an A student's goal is simple: get an A. That is what is rewarded in academia. That's all that counts. So anything that's not straight ahead toward that goal, that singular focus, tends not to be worth much of anything to an A student. And many times, because A students are so singularly focused, they completely miss seeing risk at all. Extra credit was created for A students, not C students. It is set up to maintain an A grade. An A student gets a C on a quiz he forgot to write down in his schedule. Or the dreaded pop quiz. Wham—a C on that one. Well, call in the reserves. The fall back. The "that's okay, I'll just do an extra credit report (a way to water down that mistake) so I can maintain my A average."

Because what is my goal as an A student? To get As, naturally. What is a pop quiz? It's everyday life. As Ferris Bueller says in the ultimate C student movie: "Life moves pretty fast. If you don't stop and look around once in a while, you could miss it." So here's the radical thought: Stopping and looking around is risky. *Life is risky.* But what do A students do? Everything they can to avoid risk! So they train themselves—that's right, train themselves—to actually avoid life.

And the American education system encourages this process. Academia is a bubble. It is not a real world. And academia is self-supporting. Top colleges require that everyone strives to get what the education system sells: A grades. So is it any surprise that the artificial world of academia creates an artificial measure of what success is? How do you know that if you have really good SAT scores you can actually contribute economically to yourself, to a group/company, or to the community at large? There is simply no way of connecting value and grades—unless some artificial world like academia declares value = grades. And that's crap.

So life is risky. Who doesn't know that? But what is actually risky about it? War? Of course. Global warming? Sure. But there are a billion little things that contain risk in everyday life. And the education system attempts to translate success in school into success at avoiding risk in life, which is translated into a kind of success. That's why most of America's schools are telling their students a *big fat lie* about the American dream: get As in school, go to a top college, then get a good job with a good company, get a big house and drive a nice car.

So what does that get you? As Robert Kiyosaki says in *Rich Dad, Poor Dad*, if you pursue that path you are now working for a) the government to pay your taxes, b) the bank to pay for your house and car, and c) your boss to make sure that next paycheck comes in to cover (a) and (b) above. Get it? It's a trap! All our lives we are fed this envy about good grades, great college degree, great company to work for, big house, fast car. So we lock ourselves into the big American lie. We are actually taught to run away from risk. We try to pass along that risk to our employer. We trade this fake dream for a paycheck. And as we have all seen from the vicious economic downturn in 2008 and 2009, taking a paycheck may be more risky than anyone ever dreamed, because paychecks can be taken away. And I'm saying "we," because I grew up an A student and fell into taking the paycheck dream.

And since A students are groomed by parents and teachers so early to pursue what they are good at—getting A grades—then sadly many A students are set on a course toward this risk-averse world I just described. Many A students just won't tolerate very much risk because they/we are so geared up to run away from it so early in any process. Running to safety is what it's all about. If I do an extra credit report, will you let me keep my job? Hmmm, sorry, we're not in Kansas anymore; we're trying to stay profitable.

But not the C student that sees academia for what it is and sees reasonable risk as opportunity. In years gone by, there was typically a time of recognition in a C student's life that school was not his or her arena, that success should be pursued elsewhere. But not today, not in the era of "everyone is an A student in something." The education system actually fights the C student's recognition of true standing, giving him or her As and Bs to lure him or her into the risk-averse path of the honor roll student. Young C students are not yet practiced in the art of translating risk into opportunity. But in their guts, they know—you know—that what the A students are pursuing is not what you want.

You know you should work hard in school, but what is the goal or goals that will bring you success later in life? Yes, you should work hard, but at what? Why is it important that I get an A in chemistry? How is that going to help me in life? When am I going to use chemistry in my life? Chances are you are not. So use chemistry for developing your logical, reasoning mind. Work hard to balance those equations. Yes, potassium and sodium balance each other in cell membrane activity. Balance. Ying and yang. Logic and reason.

Risk. Don't fear it…study it, embrace it, manage it. Seeing risk and managing it as opportunity is a major key to success. Embracing risk as opportunity is a key fork in the success paths taken by entrepreneurial C students that start and run their own businesses as employers versus the rest of us as employees. It is the great divider.

CHAPTER 10:

THINK AND CREATE REVENUE GENERATION (AND HIRE EXPENSE CONTROL)

So what's the most important factor in a business? Really? If you had to choose one item that you could not be in business without, what would it be?

Sales revenue. That's dollars going into the cash register. Sales.

Sure, if your costs exceed sales revenues for an extended period of time, then you don't have a business. But almost all companies start up with costs exceeding sales revenues and lose money short term. And in some years during the typical economic cycle many fine companies may lose money where revenues fall short of expenses. But without revenues, a business does not exist at all.

And where does sales revenue come from?

It comes from other people. Third parties. Customers. People who have been convinced your product or service is worthy of them reaching into their pockets and giving you cash for what you have to offer. If you really think about it, the process is extraordinary. Why do people choose to purchase *any* particular product or service? Reasons run the gambit. But one thing is for sure: if you are able to generate sales revenues, you will probably do well.

In general, people that figure out how to generate sales revenues are the creators of business in America and in the world—literally. Most accounting and law firms don't create business. They support them. Revenue generators hire accountants and lawyers to control costs and excessive risks while the business creator goes out and generates sales dollars. But wait…there are accounting firms and law firms, aren't there? Sure. Those groups that are really good at controlling costs and minimizing risk for business customers grow and flourish. But here's a really interesting point about accounting firms and law firms: The leaders of these firms typically don't actually do much actual accounting or legal work. No, they don't. Rather, the head muckety muck of the big law firm in Dallas or accounting firm in New York tends to spend all his or her time selling. That's right. Their job is to go out and sell the services of the firm—to generate sales revenue.

So what does all this mean to a sixteen- or seventeen-year-old? What it means is that if you want to be successful, then you need to learn how to generate revenue. So how do you do that? In the next chapter, I'll recommend the summer jobs you should pursue from now until you are twenty-two. And that's going to be hard. Some summers you may not make any money at all. And your parents may get angry. They may argue that you need to generate income to help pay for college or gas or car insurance. But if you take a long-term vision of why you do the jobs you do when you are sixteen to twenty-two, it will pay great dividends after school.

Okay, but, you say, what do I do about my C+ average right now? I hate chemistry and don't understand what the War of 1812 has to do with anything about generating revenue or doing anything this book is suggesting. Maybe…but maybe not. Let's look at the revenue generating businessperson again. He or she has started a service business or is making a product. Where did the idea come from? Was it just a knack that person had for creative ideas? Everyone has ideas. So why was *that* idea so successful? How do you get from having an idea, understanding it is a good idea and not just an everyday idea, refine it, and set about putting the idea into the market place in order to generate revenue to create real business? That is really hard. And it's almost impossible for you to do if you are locked into a system set up to serve other people (i.e. your boss).

It is easier to go along to get along and get a good job, to fall into the trap so well described in Robert

Kiyosaki's *Rich Dad, Poor Dad*: get good grades, go to a good school, get a good job, and buy a house and car with big monthly payments. Locked into the system working for someone else with fake economic security. The American dream? Hardly.

What you should be doing with your C+ average is enjoying school. Huh? But you say you hate school. You can't wait to get out. Quitting has crossed your mind more than once. Is this all there is? You think you're bad at school and it's a dead end. I will grant you the reasons laid out in this book have not been told to too many C+ students over the past hundred years. I would say almost none.

But the successful C students somehow figured it out on their own with a nudge from a thoughtful person in their lives: that to be successful, someone has to go out and take a risk. Start something to fulfill a need. Generate sales revenue. And no book is going to teach you that. And certainly no middle school or high school is going to encourage that path. Hopefully a teacher, parent, or friend encourages you to understand this fundamental concept.

Generating sales revenue comes from two things: 1) rational, logical thought processes, and 2) actually getting out there and doing it. And the reason you are in school is to teach your brain rational, logical thought processes. NOT to learn chemistry or the events of the War of 1812. And teaching your brain rational, logical thought takes a long time and is built on a foundation of K-8 fundamentals.

Think revenue generation. How do you convince Joe Consumer to actually buy something? Pick up the LL Bean and J Crew catalogs or any other two comparable catalogs that come to your house. How are those products any different from each other? Why does someone buy the shoes from LL Bean or J Crew? Is it just price? Why does someone buy a Nissan or a Ford when it's just transportation? *Is* it just transportation?

These are not really business questions in the sense that you need to go to business school to understand them. Well, many people go to a business school to understand them. But those schools often fall into the same trap of seeking the A student. Are those the best business candidates? Or are they the best candidates to grow and support existing businesses? It's been my experience that great businesspeople are great revenue generators. And great revenue generation is not taught in school. It's learned *out there* by people willing to take a risk—C students.

The yearning to do something more than school work is the key point in time for many successful young adults. Which is why this book is written for fourteen- to eighteen-year-olds with a C average (or what should be a C average). I'm pretty sure your guidance counselor hasn't given you the message laid out in this book: that America's future is largely dependent on a bunch of you C students rocking the economic world so that many of us A and B students can remain gainfully employed! And the rest of the population, for that matter. After all, according to a recent ad I saw from Sprint, sixty-four percent of all new jobs since 1995 were created by small businesses. So it is critical to our economy that some of you must realize that you have to go out on your own and start a business. And this book is insisting you look at the remaining days of high school and four years of college differently than everyone else is telling you to: as you take your classes, learn how to think about sales revenue generation in the business world. Actually, let me shorten that for now: *learn how to think.*

Saying that learning how to think is tantamount to success is likely to be taken as an insult by a teenager. But please don't take it that way. Rather, take it as an escape from what everyone else has told you about school: that revenue generators and profit makers, the truly successful people in the world, have sharpened their ability to think more clearly than the rest of the population. And that talent isn't reflected in grades. Rather, I am suggesting, perhaps for the first time you've ever heard it, not to think of school work as school work. Don't think of chemistry as chemistry. Think of it as practice. Learning how to identify patterns on partial information. Practice. It's not chemistry. It's the brain learning one single lesson: how to take the risk to get from point A to point B without really getting hurt.

And that's the key to school—mental exercise, and the brain of a typical sixteen- or seventeen-year-old is terribly out of shape. It doesn't matter which exercise you choose, it's going to hurt at first. The brain is going to resist just like any muscle in your body resists a tiring exercise. Because it hurts a little. But if you have a coach—maybe this book—that you trust, that tells you if you exercise every day then your brain is going to get into terrific shape.

And getting your brain into terrific shape is not going to make it smarter. You are not going to be able to regurgitate dates and events leading up to the French Revolution or whatever. But what you are going to be able to do is discuss *why* the French Revolution occurred or the American Revolution, or *why* people buy Nike products or super size their fries, because you now understand *why* you are studying in high school.

Brain conditioning means preparing you to become a revenue generator. You may end up hiring the valedictorian of your graduating class to represent you in the lawsuit to protect your company's patent. Revenue generation and then profit making. It makes the world go around.

Here are some real life examples:

My cousin in Florida (I'll call him Roy), who barely made it through a state university, took over his family's business after his dad's tragic death in an airplane accident. He struggled to understand the company, fought off the bankers, identified revenue-generation opportunities, got really smart people to help him control expenses, re-righted the ship, grew revenues substantially, and sold the company several years later. He and his family made millions. The buy-out firm that purchased his company was made up of really smart guys. Big name school MBAs. Money firm from New York, and they were rolling up similar companies. Going to create a bigger and better company by collecting all those companies into a single company and save money by eliminating double efforts, etc.

One problem: the new owners didn't know how to generate revenue. The customer was assumed. That is, the financial buyers never really understood why customers bought Roy's product. It was assumed the customers would keep buying while the new owners focused on really cool ways to cut costs.

And the company tanked.

And Roy bought it back at a fraction of what he sold it for.

And Roy went back out to see his customers and started generating revenue again.

And he just sold the company again for millions more.

He knew *why* his customers bought his product, and he also took care of his customers and understood the way they think. Revenue generation.

Here's another real story:

A local company in New England makes a metal product, one that's used all over the world, and one that you would not think would be fabricated in New England. The owner reached the age of forty, and wanting to spend more time with his wife and kids while they were young, he sold his company to a bunch of really smart guys—money guys. They kept him on as president and brought in a finance guy. But they made the finance guy a notch above the president; they made the finance guy "chief executive."

The new chief executive didn't have a clue about how a dollar of revenue was generated. He just wanted to control costs…such as severely reducing inventory because having all that stuff in the warehouse cost money. The chief executive communicated almost exclusively by e-mail. Never went to see a customer. So when one of the biggest companies in the world called in a rush order—a product that used to be carried in the warehouse—the company lost an initial small sale that could have turned into a very large sale. Hundreds of thousands of dollars in revenue lost because the first $10,000 sale could not be made.

Frustrated, the former owner, as president, quit. He could not work for a company that couldn't reason through a logical thought process to understand what it meant to generate revenue. Smart guys, A students, wrecking in three years what it took a C student fifteen years of sweat and blood to create.

It happens all the time.

CHAPTER 11:

YOUR BEST SUMMER JOB

"I wish every worker in America had to be a freelancer at selling or writing or painting or carpentry or computer repair or law or something for two years. I wish Americans could have a period in their lives when they only got paid for what they sold or produced. It would do this country a world of good." Ben Stein (quoting his friend Mike)

An Indian (from India) friend of mine told me about a family practice in his culture that is not widely known: they pay each other to hire each other's children. Of course the youngsters don't know their uncle or aunt has been paid to hire them. But rather than have a son or daughter immediately come into a business as the "owner's son" or "owner's daughter," that kid is thrust into an environment where he or she must please someone other than Mom or Dad. That kid is out selling and getting the education of his or her life working for an uncle that is never satisfied, teaching his nephew or niece what it really means to succeed.

This particular practice in a segment of the Indian culture believes that entrepreneurship comes from truly understanding what it means to generate a revenue dollar—not counting that dollar, not managing that dollar. Nope. *Making* a dollar. What it takes is to get other people to let go of that dollar...take it out of their pockets and give it...to you. To keep. Forever, if you'd like. Because now that dollar is yours, in exchange for some product or service those people purchased. Or that you sold to them.

Sales. It's what most people fear the most, because it is risky. But it is what must occur so that everyone else gets paid.

So how is a dollar of revenue generated? Using a sports analogy, if it appears that it's easy for Manny Ramirez to hit a baseball, it's not. Or Tom Glavine to throw that nasty slider. It takes a lot of work. They have spent years perfecting the art of what they do. And so do people in the business world. And in my opinion, the best way to see the path to success is to force yourself to take that dreaded position of a salesperson early in life—a commissioned salesperson with no certainty of a pay check.

What? No certain income? But I need to make $X this summer to pay for my car insurance! Well then, go ahead. And fall into the false security game. Fall into mediocrity. But for those of you reading this that will actually take this advice, go get a sales job next summer, or even better, after school during the school year. Sell anything: plastic pipe or carpet. Go sell grass seed. It doesn't matter.

And if you get that job in sales, then you will learn what some people in my friend's culture actually pay for: that generating a revenue dollar is the hardest and most rewarding thing to do. It's not that you have to be a salesperson your whole life, but rather truly understand where a dollar of revenue comes from, and this takes actually doing it. And those that master that art and then build around that knowledge will lead wonderfully successful lives.

Think about what my friend's culture is saying: I will pay my brother, just as I would pay a college, to teach my daughter or son how to do something. But my daughter or son does not know I am paying my brother. My child is sent off to my brother's hotel to sell hotel rooms or catering or meeting room space on the phone, in person, and/or at the front desk. And my son or daughter will feel the pain of *failing*, experience the ire of an angry guest, and feel the exhilaration of solving a tough situation on their feet and at that moment. It might be two a.m. and no one else is up at the hotel. The hotel is full. And a traveling business-man comes into the lobby with a confirmed late arrival reservation. Oh my goodness. My nineteen-year-old is in troooouuubbbble. Good. Because that is what life is all about in the world of solving for success. Where is the solution in this seemingly impossible situation? Solving for X.

And this friend of mine and his family are tremendously successful. And their children will be too. They understand and will pass along an understanding of how to generate a revenue dollar.

The most successful person in my high school class sold carpet on commission during his summers. I life guarded...because that's where the girls were. He was a C student and ran the football pool in the school cafeteria. I took calculus my junior year and graduated first in my class. He owns thousands of apartments across the U.S. and flies privately. I do not.

So what is it about selling that make young C students successful and why the rest of us fear it so much?

1. Selling is really hard and takes an incredible amount of finesse and preparation. Being turned down most of the time is a big part of selling. And it takes a lot of guts to be able to get turned down a lot.
2. *Everyone* in an organization is completely dependent upon the people that bring the revenue through the door. And that's a lot of pressure. But in good companies (especially your own), that effort is handsomely rewarded. It's not the product that sells, although good products are critical to good sales. Rather, it is

people—salespeople—that bring people into the process of letting go of their precious dollars. All other jobs in an organization, such as accountants, janitors, lawyers, are all dependent upon salespeople that take a risk every day to generate revenue.

3. Knowing how to sell/what it takes to sell is a big key to a successful life, because it teaches you what is important: make sure that people are happy with what they receive. And once you understand how to do that, then you are ready to be successful. That might be owning your own company, but whatever it is, you finally... finally...get it.

III.
The Average Student Solution:

Stop Chasing A's if You're not Already
There. Because in Real Life, Many
A Students end up Working
for C Students

CHAPTER 12:

JUST LET GO.

Chase Your Own Dreams, Not Someone Else's

"Follow your dreams, because you are going to be dead for a very, very, very long time." H. Timothy O'Neil

My wife is friends with a famous comedian. Or was. They grew up together. She tells our kids he was her first boyfriend. Then they tease me about wishing he was their dad...that they would then be rich and famous. I'm not sure about the boyfriend part, but I do know they were good friends in high school. I first met "Joe" in church. Catholic church. Midnight mass on Christmas Eve. My wife and I had just driven in from Washington and drove straight to mass in the Philadelphia area. My wife's old high school gang was there, and she introduced me to her friends, including Joe, in communion line. The problem is Joe is Jewish. So his position in line on the way to receiving Catholic communion made me a little nervous.

As we progressed toward the priest handing out communion—pretty close to the front row—Joe turned back to me as he stepped out of line at the last second and said, "I was just looking for a better seat."

I am told Joe wanted to be a professional soccer player when he was in high school. He went on to a great college. He majored in a science and came back home. I'm also told Joe tried the soccer route, but apparently it did not work out. I'm not sure what Joe starting doing for a day job, but his natural calling of comedy started pulling him into New York City. He started doing stand up—the typical route of most comedians. We went to see him a couple of times over the early years. And since then, we have gone to New York to see his show and spent some time afterwards in his office with his gumball machine and all the other gadgets of a comedic madman.

But despite having spent a little time with such a great talent and having a wife that knew him well at one time, I actually learned more about Joe's success in an interview I read about him somewhere. Someone asked him when he realized he was going to make it in the entertainment industry. His reply was something like, "I didn't. But I can tell you that (my success) started as soon as I let go of everything else and started doing comedy full time." (For the record, Joe was an honor roll student and not a C student, proving once again that generalizations tend to be wrong. And hopefully it may also suggest that A students could gain something from this book.)

Letting go. What is that, anyway? People have all kinds of analogies: I stopped keeping one foot on the dock with the other on the boat as it pulled away. Quitting your day job. Stuff like that. I think letting go means commitment. A commitment to yourself and what you really want to pursue. What you really want to do. What will make you happy and fulfilled. Whatever that is. C.S. Lewis wrote this line about a character talking at the end of his life: "I just realized I spent my whole life neither doing what I should have done nor what I wanted to do." I think that's most of us, because most of us have followed a path set out for us by other people instead of taking the reasonable risk and following our own gut of what will really make us successful.

I am using the Joe story in the full context of his experience up to the point of his "letting go." He was a very well-educated young man. He obtained a liberal arts degree. Yes, it was from a great school, and while my bet is Joe wouldn't trade his top college experience for the world, it is also my bet he'd encourage everyone and anyone to pursue a college education *wherever* they can get it. Community college...wherever. Just get that college education anywhere, because it really doesn't matter where. What matters is that your brain is fully exercised and ready to think rationally when you make that, well, risky move to try to do what you really want to do. To let go.

Of course, I'm being provocative when I say a "risky move." As it is with any risk, the pursuit of a passion in life must be thoughtfully weighed. And in order for it to be weighed correctly, a rational mind must weigh it. Logic must be on your side. And you must have thought about risk in a positive, opportunistic light as we discuss throughout in this book. Most people view the letting go moment as too risky. And that's largely cultural. And I believe that risk aversion is taught in our schools. We are programmed not to let go. We are taught to do what others think is the right thing. Be safe. Stay the course. Be the Poor Dad and get a good job, a mortgage, pay taxes...and live life at break-even instead of going for it...and truly being successful.

So what happens when you get to that point when you actually let go? In reality, I think most rational people prepare for that point. It is not a "wake up and do it" kind of thing. I've watched and heard the story many times. Someone like a friend of mine that runs her own insurance agency in New Hampshire. Recently I was standing next to her watching our boys take batting practice. We turned to the subject of try-outs and making a team. And that turned to business. So I asked her about her story.

She now has over five thousand clients served out of a small office in a small retail center. She employs three salespeople full time. Benefits, bonuses, the whole nine yards. Small business America. "Jerry" says she barely made it out of high school. She was told she needed to get better at typing, because that's all she could probably do (Have you heard this before?). She settled into a nice little job at a local grocery store in Illinois—small town America. Had a nice car and apartment. And someone she trusted suggested she look at the insurance industry. Interested, she became a claims person—it had a salary just like her grocery store job.

After a few months, she heard about how much the commissioned agents made. Lots and lots. Agency was where the money was. And Jerry knew. She knew she wanted more in her life than her paycheck to pay the rent, taxes, and car payment. She wanted nice things. She wanted to provide for a family. But how? She shared this desire to let go of a salary position in order to really reach for her dreams with her now husband "Rich." They were dating. Rich had a nice job. So did Jerry. Could they live off his salary while she picked up an agency? When a move to New England for Rich presented itself, they went for it. Jerry opened an agency office in New Hampshire and a new business, and an old dream became reality. Jerry let go. The C student living and building the American dream. She is now an employer, not an employee. She has a growing business. The C student fulfilling the American dream.

Two brothers lost two gyms and borrowed $20,000 before making it big with one of the most successful franchise businesses in America today. By 2010, they had close to one hundred employees and over 350 franchises all over the country. They let go of the notion they could only be successful slugging it out locally. I don't know for sure, but my bet is the brothers were not A students. But they studied the key risks of the fitness industry, meaning cash flow and customer retention, and developed systems to far out-perform the industry.

Let me be clear: letting go is not jumping off a cliff. It does not mean being reckless. It comes from a desire to stop living other people's dreams and expectations about what they think is a fulfilling life for you and start pursuing what you want to do. But it is a reasoned approach. It is a logical approach. It is thought out. Is it risky? Sure. Almost everything worthwhile in life contains some level of risk. Medical breakthroughs (what did the establishment think of the guy who suggested stomach ulcers were caused by bacteria?) or starting a new business. But knowing that it is okay to seek out reasonable risk is ninety percent of the game. Knowing that other foreign cultures actually promote it within their subcultures. Knowing that it is okay to let go of other's expectations and start expecting from yourself.

Go to college. Get your mind fully exercised so it can weigh risk and opportunity properly, logically.

Create a dream. Prepare for that time. And then let go.

"Imagination is more important than knowledge." Albert Einstein

CHAPTER 13:

GO TO COLLEGE – NO MATTER WHAT

I hope a lot of people reading this book don't stop reading at this point, put it down without finishing and conclude I don't think people should go to college. That's not true. I think *everyone* should go to college, no matter what it takes. And the good news is that education is now such an oversold business that there is a college for everyone to attend at almost any price level. This is contrary to the latest trendy thinking; people like Charles Murray in *Real Education* that say college for many is a waste of time. Hog wash. That's training vs. brain surgeon mindset: If you're not an A student, then go get some vocational training. This kills me. Why are the intellectual elite so lost when it comes to what an education is really all about? According to Thomas Stanley's *The Millionaire's Mind,* ninety percent of the millionaires he surveyed went to college. But to confirm what I am saying here, Dr. Stanley reports that millionaires that own their own businesses are typically C students. Their average GPA in college? 2.76.

So I have some news for you: You can be successful attending any college and being a C student so long as you strive hard for your own internal goals and not the external goals of the system. Don't worry about missing out on the top school track; not everyone going to the top fifty colleges is going to light up the world or get rich. And not everyone going to the top fifty colleges is going to become happy and financially independent. And I am willing to bet the majority of those going to a top fifty college never end up starting a business and/or working for themselves.

I went to Georgetown. Some call it a top school. And most of my friends from Georgetown have made good money, and some have significant wealth. But almost none of them started their own business or are working for themselves. They are big Wall Street guys and gals or muckety mucks in XYZ Company… but it's not their company. And that's because most of us were A students in high school. And most of us were trained to be risk averse in order to get into Georgetown. I currently work for a C student, and I have for most of the jobs I have had in my career. Sure, I've done okay, but I've not *really done* anything.

So forget not going to college if you can't go to a top college. *Go to college. Period.* The reason everyone should go to college is because the current high school format is not thorough enough to truly educate you. Remember I am not talking about a particular subject. I am talking about preparing your mind in a thorough manner to allow you to function outside the academic world in a rational, problem solving manner. Sounds easy, but it isn't. It takes hard work to become a self-actualizing human being. That's why four years of college is so important—a high school diploma is just getting started with your mind, but unlike one hundred years ago, your cake is just half baked by high school graduation day.

When you get to college, including a liberal arts college if you so choose, funny things start to happen in your classes: the same names, events, and theories start to be mentioned in multiple classes. Isaac Newton was a scientist, a mathematician, and a philosopher. So were John Stuart Mill...and Jefferson...and...and. Pretty soon you realize there is something going on that you've never seen before: the underlying thought process that these great people used must have some commonality, something you do not yet have but that the school you are attending is dangling in front of you. But no one says anything. It just goes on. And then...there it is again...in economics class...in sociology class...in whatever class. What is going on? What is this secret that everyone else knows except me?!

And then they really mess you up. They introduce you to a class called philosophy and to the Greeks. People you may have heard of like Socrates, Plato, and Aristotle. And the teacher starts talking about concepts like justice. Pretty easy concept, right? Until you realize the smartest of the smart guys can't really pin down a definition. *Really?* But we have an entire system called a justice system—how can smart guys like Socrates not be able to clearly define it?

And so it hits you...your first real thinking challenge. Sure, you've had tough problems before, in chemistry or algebra or whatever class. But now you are presented with a real life example of "no right answer." Sure there is. Isn't there?

So you are saying to yourself, how do I as a young kid figure out something that the smartest guys in the world couldn't figure out? And again, no one tells you that this is what occurs every day in life, the challenges facing businesses and governments and scientists every day. Imagine the point in time when people began to say the earth was round and not flat. Or that the earth was not the center of the universe. Imagine coming up with some ideas like that today? Yet it happens every day. How? Logical thought. Something somewhere doesn't quite fit. Of course the world had to be round and the earth was not the center of the universe—we know that now. But for a very long time, very smart people could not figure it out. But logic prevailed.

And it is through this process of reasoned thought that most problems are solved, most profits are made, and most lives are saved (stomach ulcers were just recently discovered to be caused by bacteria and treatable with antibiotics. No way! Way). And without properly educated minds, we tend not to think logically. We are not naturally reasoning beings—or at least we are no longer being taught to be so. Without reason, we react emotionally or we mimic people we perceive as knowledgeable. We become regurgitators of truisms and platitudes. We don't really understand these statements posed to us as facts—they just become common thought if we say them enough. Sure, we get the basics: I'm hungry therefore I need something to eat. But as the concepts get more and more complicated and harder to solve, the logical sequences and the reasoning becomes harder and harder as well. Your mind needs a) a strong foundation and b) strong reasoning skills in order to tackle complex problems. Otherwise we simply react emotionally or fall into group-think (a reason why politics today are so polarized).

So college is a finishing place of what high school started. And it provides more time to allow that to happen in your life. Not in a particular subject, but in developing your mind to think more logically... rationally...clearly. How to organize and then simplify complex thoughts. How to debate competing opinions and perspectives. And ultimately how to benefit yourself and others from the solutions you develop.

CHAPTER 14:

GO WITH THE FLOW.
DON'T FIGHT THE TIDE

"The problem is we all try to go north in the southbound lane."
Don Imus

All too often, immature minds, including my own, believe that in order to be really creative or successful, one must come up with that revolutionary idea that will change the world or completely change the way people do business. In reality, it is the savvy mind that thinks of complementing the existing flow, such as capitalizing on the movement of services or goods already moving in a particular direction. Grand inventions or discoveries are indeed rare. It is very hard or almost impossible to swim against a tide for very long.

Don't do it.

Let's use the iPod as an example. Music downloading was not new. And MP3 players were not knew. Apple knew the industry was moving and in fact had already significantly moved in the direction of consumers getting their music online. The problem—or actually the opportunity—was that no one was paying for that music. Web pages and services like Napster and others at the time allowed peer-to-peer file sharing, claiming such an activity should be free of charge. And billions of dollars were at stake.

Billions of dollars. That's the opportunity. No one was making billions of dollars getting in the way of a significant flow of goods and services *already occurring*.

Enter the rule of law. The problem with the system prior to iTunes was that it was illegal to download copyrighted music without paying for it. And contrary to popular opinion, people don't break the law and steal if a) they are told by a court it's illegal, and b) they might get caught, and most importantly c) they will be prosecuted and fined.

Now I have no way of knowing if Apple was involved in the early litigation involving illegal music downloading. But it's clear they were prepared. What seemed like overnight, as soon as the lawsuits started against average people downloading pirated music, the iTunes phenomenon started to happen. The web page was there with almost any music you wanted. And the price was right: ninety-nine cents. Heck, a pack of gum costs more than ninety-nine cents.

Apple saw the *existing* flow of goods and services. And Apple just got in the way. Some people say they changed the way people obtained their music, but all they did was modify the existing process and changed the public into, once again, a buying public. Prior to Napster, the public purchased music in music stores, etc., while the Napster free music era was short lived… and in many cases illegal. Logic would tell anyone that something that big and that illegal used by the general public would come to an end. Like Prohibition. But there it was: an almost insatiable desire for a product. The flow—already in existence. The market had the flow of product/services but no money. So create a virtual store. And make it compatible with a really cool gadget. Price it reasonably, but do NOT try to change the flow. Don't go to a new form of CD that holds twice as many songs or a new eight-track tape. Go with the flow. People want to download music online into portable devices. So get in the way of the flow and make gobs of money. Be smart and swim with the tide.

CHAPTER 15:

NEGATIVE PEOPLE: DON'T JUST STAY AWAY FROM NEGATIVE PEOPLE...RUN AWAY FROM THEM

Whoever said that is a genius. Because it is so true: negative people destroy more on this planet than earthquakes, fires, and volcanoes. Negativity destroys creativity and therefore deprives the rest of the world from enjoying the next big idea.

Many skeptics who have reached this point in the book will be nodding their heads up and down. "Yes, Mr. Pickett, you are such a negative person for putting down the American education system. Millions of people have worked their entire lives to better educate the children of this country and you are boldly saying they are all wrong. You, sir, are a negative person."

My response is that's a classic circle-the-wagons attitude to protect the status quo. The glass half full answer is to be positive about being a C student and exclaim from the highest mountains that it takes more than good grades and being a co-co-co-captain of the soccer team to make this world great—and I mean, great. Not nice…but *great*. We need the C students to go light this world up with their guts and risk taking. We need C students to go out and create the companies that create the jobs and the balance sheets for A students to balance and organizations for A students to organize. We need better and more efficient ways to do stuff. And C students get that done. Maybe not how to put more information onto a microchip but rather thinking of ways to get that microchip to help us in our everyday lives.

When I talk to parents of high school seniors, I get a feeling of sadness most of the time. Invariably the subject comes up: Which college is little Johnny going to? Well, it isn't Princeton. Parents aren't embarrassed, but it's kind of a denial that their child has not reached the promised land of going to that "envy" school. The hope of "one of the best" is finally dashed. Reality sets in: little Johnny is just gonna be average. That's one of the most negative things I have ever heard.

America today is the land of plenty. Plenty of small businesses. Tons of them. Almost thirty million of them. And the majority of those businesses are started by people who were considered average students when they were in high school. Every time I meet people who run their own business, I ask them how they did in high school. You try it. You'll see. These are the most positive people in the world. They wake up every morning scared to death. Scared to death to make payroll so their employees' families can eat and drive to work. Scared to death their best customers will call that day to say they found a better service provider or cheaper supplier. But these business owners are positive. Positive because somewhere along their journey a light clicked on or someone said to them—go for it. You can do it. This is America, so what's your downside? That's positive.

Negative people say "can't be done." "Too risky." "Payment is not certain." All negative... all the time. My advice? Run away from these risk-averse people. And I mean run. They will cause doubt in your own mind. They will spread their hovering gray cloud into your life and your dreams. Don't let it happen. Stay away. Run away. Stay positive. There is nothing wrong with being scared.

I hear the best actors in Hollywood are actually shy. They act to overcome their fear. Fear is a great motivator. Fear is the key ingredient to success, according to Frank Perdue. But being afraid and being negative do not go hand in hand. Rather, positive people see risk as opportunity, and they also see a certain level of fear as positive—if it wasn't thrilling, then why do it? Roller coasters, race car driving, parachuting. Fun? Yes. Terrifying? Yes. Positive experience? You bet.

"Optimism is fun, healthy, and empowering." Bert Jacobs, cofounder of Life is Good.

CHAPTER 16

HAVE A PLAN

"There are no good jobs, only good opportunities." Paul Walsh

I know I have referenced this book a few times, but one of the best books for kids to read today is *Rich Dad Poor Dad* by Robert Kiyosaki. In summary, I believe his message is not too dissimilar to this book: if you are not careful, you will fall for what the system wants you to do, and then you are trapped. Kiyosaki describes the big trap: get good grades, go to a good college, get a good job, buy a house with a big mortgage, drive a nice car with a big car payment…and you are in a big hole. Now if you follow this path, you are then working for three people: 1) making money for your boss because you need the next paycheck he gives you to pay for all your possessions, 2) the bank, for whom you are working to pay your mortgage and car payment, and 3) you are working for the government to pay your taxes. You are broke every morning. You have to go to work, or else someone comes and takes your goodies away from you.

What kind of life is that? Answer: a lot of people live like that in America. A lot of really smart people. Some call it the American dream: big title at work, big house, fancy car, and nice dress shirts. Kiyosaki calls it effectively the big American lie. It's what the system has sold you—you were supposed to do all that...now what?

Don't fall for it. Instead, have a plan. As another great author, Stephen Covey, says: begin with the end in mind. In a perfect world, where do you want to end up? I think most people would say working for themselves with enough money in the bank not to worry about day-to-day economics and for their children's education costs and retirement. Kiyosaki calls this financial independence—not reliant on anyone or any system for income or retirement. And in order to achieve that, at any age, one must have a plan. How to get from point A to point B. And I have given you some of the early points in that plan:

- Understand why you are in school
- understand where a dollar of revenue really comes from
- learn how to generate revenue in your early employment years

In summary, have a goal, look for the opportunity, understand the risk, and go for it. Most people are afraid of opportunity, believing there is too much risk to pursue it. But it is the C student that says, why not? This is America. What's my downside? So I start over if I fail. *I've done that before...I know it's possible.* I'll embrace that reasonable risk as an opportunity to eventually become my own boss any day.

CHAPTER 17:

PUTTING IT ALL TOGETHER:

The reason you are in school: In order to be success-ful in the world today, you must be decisive in a risky environment.

Wow, that's it? Yep, that's it. But it is harder than it seems. And the primary reasons why it's harder than it seems are as follows:

- <u>We are taught not to take risk</u>. "A" students, as you have learned, actually become risk averse in their effort to please a teacher or parent and to understand everything as they strive to achieve the almighty A. Risk is therefore bad...at almost any level.

- <u>No one likes to be wrong</u>. And the only way to be wrong is if you make a decision. That's why many people learn ways not to make deci-sions...because they don't want to be wrong. Think about this for a second. Bureaucracies are entire institutions set up to make sure no one within the organization has to make a decision. The system operates on automatic. People are simply cogs in the machine—risk free. In this way, no one is ever wrong but simply doing what they are told *by the system*.

- <u>Partial Information.</u> Most people have poor decision making skills. As a result, they constantly seek more and more information in order to avoid making a mistake and being wrong. In the meantime, the opportunity disappears—and a better decision maker snatches it up.

"I can name that tune...in three notes."

If you are in eighth or ninth grade, you've probably never heard someone say something like the above. But your parents probably have. Back in the 1970 and '80s, there was a television show called *Name That Tune.* Contestants would try to out-duel each other by predicting they could name the next song in fewer and fewer notes. And the lowest bid (in number of notes) was allowed to stump the host.

The game is a classic example of what it means to put everything together from your education. The whole purpose of education is to develop one's mind to come to a conclusion or, more importantly, make a decision based on partial information. And the one that is able to make the correct decision—not guess—based on the least amount of certain information typically wins in life.

So how does one make decisions based upon partial information?

Vast amounts of learned knowledge? Possible but not probable.

Experience? Yes...to some extent.

A reasoned process of thought based on reasonable connections based on a sound foundation? Yes.

The best combination? A reasonable, rational mind combined with experience. This is the definition of a wise person.

In the book *Real Education*, Charles Murray describes this as "Rigor in Forming Judgments" and lists four key components that allow someone to develop sound judgment:

1) "Having a flair for making sense of complicated situations"

He mentions common sense as part of this flair, but I believe he incorrectly states that this trait is un-teachable. Further, I believe he incorrectly relates this trait as being "surely correlated with academic ability."

I would argue common sense, street smarts, and any other label one chooses to put on this flair are actually taught every day...through failure. True, making sense of complicated situations is more than common sense, but it has been my experience that many academically gifted people tend to experience more complications by constantly seeking more data instead of simplification. "Paralysis by analysis" is a common problem for the academically gifted. In their efforts to eliminate risk in a complicated situation, the academically gifted more often than not grind to a halt as they attempt to gain more and more information while seeking the risk-free solution. This is because they have never failed or have rarely been allowed to experience failure.

The real C student experiences failure all the time. And through practice, the C student learns how to simplify complicated situations into concepts and steps he or she can actually succeed at—and then sets about executing those steps. And what is most important is that the C student moves forward without the need to eliminate all risk by attempting to gather all possible information related to the topic.

2) "Appropriate application of logic"

Once again, Mr. Murray implies that this characteristic is the domain of the gifted. Logic is not taught in many of our schools, but it should be. And I would argue that C students can gain sufficient logic through a solid education in order to appropriately apply it in complicated situations (such as simplifying rather than getting bogged down in detail or missing information – see #1 above).

3) "Evaluation of data"

The best analysts are the academically gifted. Financial analysts on Wall Street. Lawyers. Doctors. Rocket scientists. However, I would argue that this ability is not necessary to develop sound judgment if one can hire an analyst to disaggregate components of a complicated situation and allow the decision maker to efficiently translate those bits of information in an analysis. In fact, smart business owners do this all the time. It is sound judgment for a business owner to hire an academically gifted lawyer when his or her business is sued. Hire that top talent to evaluate data.

4) "Pattern recognition"

Mr. Murray comes very close to recognizing "risk taking" by citing this trait, but I believe he falls short. A willingness to take a risk to seize an opportunity is essential to success. Pattern recognition is meaningless if someone cannot then do something about the pattern—before the pattern is fully played out for everyone else to see. In the book *The Outliers*, Malcolm Gladwell cites a study of professional card players' superior ability to recognize patterns subconsciously— before they even realize they have recognized a pattern! Risk takers...

So I believe that throughout his excellent book Mr. Murray ignores a fundamental success trait needed yet lacking in our education system: the ability to face possible failure and step forward to progress in the face of risk. I will call this "Big #5."

5) Learn How to Take Risk

Risk taking is absent from Mr. Murray's *Real Education*. I have not done an electronic word search, but in my visual scanning of the book, I could not find the word "risk" used even a single time. This character trait, I believe, is the culmination of the four traits described by Murray. Success in life is based on the ability to see risk, understand risk, and make decisions within a risky environment. And a history of failure, correction, and pressing forward wiser and more experienced from that failure is *necessary* for success in life. And more often than not, the C student is best positioned to gain that type of experience.

The opposite of this successful formula of being decisive in a risky environment is bureaucracy. My definition of bureaucracy is a system set up within which no decisions or progress is made. Some see these bureaucracies, such as government entities and those that run them, as leaders of our country and way of life. I see small businesses and their owners as the center of our country. They are the job creators, our engines of success.

Look at how bureaucracies work (or don't work) and protect themselves. They play the game of no decision even in the way they interact with the people they serve. Often legislation and laws are written using what is referred to as "choice architecture." This technique seeks to establish the default position as what these bureaucracies want as an outcome: lulling people into making no decisions for themselves and their own futures. Treat people as sheep and allow that treatment to be self-fulfilling. "We the bureaucracy will take care of you...make no decision...be passive... the system is right, and we will take care of you." How in the world does that bring any type of happiness or fulfillment? It doesn't.

In terms of the conclusions you may draw from this book, I believe a great deal of happiness and fulfillment can come from being at peace with being a C student. When you stop and think about it, chasing As is really someone else's goal. Being at peace with what you do best, and pursuing it, brings inner peace.

Most people chase a college degree to get a job and the certainty of a paycheck—as if that is ever a certainty today. And most of the time it's to please their parents...to eliminate uncertainty in their own late-stage lives, not in the life of the student. Instead, young people should go to college for the development of a logical and rational mind in order to help mature their minds to evaluate and judge risk. Anything else is just training to work for someone else.

In the *New York Times'* "Career Couch" article by Eilene Zimmerman on October 25, 2009, Ms. Zimmerman asks, "Why expect a 17-year-old to stay on one path?" Joan E. McLean at Ohio Wesleyan says, "Part of guiding high school juniors and seniors toward their calling is allowing them to find their calling, to see what best suits their still developing values and interests."

And the last place one finds those values and interests in the average kid is in grade point averages.

A final word should be said about wise decision making or sound judgment. What is not often mentioned in wise decision making or sound judgment is: know what you don't know. Seek help in areas unfamiliar to you. But don't guess and make stupid mistakes. And don't be indecisive if a critical piece of information or knowledge is missing. Go get it, plug it in, and then decide. Sadly, our education system teaches none of this. Instead, A students seek to be know-it-all decision makers, avoiding risk at all costs, and satisfying other people's goals.

At the other end, we fail to recognize our dependence on successful risk takers—our savvy C students—to bring jobs to our local economies…and thus our national economies, which are necessary for our American way of life to survive.

EPILOGUE

I hope you enjoyed the book. Here is my C student cheat sheet:

Know why you are doing what you are doing.

Know the fundamentals...cold. Practice, practice, practice.

Success is habit forming. And good habits come from practice.

Simplify...work hard to break down complicated issues into two to three major focus points.

Have a plan
Execute your plan
Learn and then amend plan
Finish
Follow-up
Repeat

Always show up ready and on time.

Ninety percent of success is just showing up.

Know what you don't know.

Always finish exhausted.

Know time management.

4 Key skills to gain from K-12 education:

1) Read at a true twelfth-grade level;
2) Write at a true twelfth-grade level.
3) Know basic math in your head: addition, subtraction, multiplication and division up to 12 x 12. Fractions and decimals too.
4) Become comfortable speaking in front of small groups (say ten or less).

Pause and ask yourself, "Is my response/answer/action rational and logical or emotionally driven?"

Recognize risk but do not fear it. Understand risk as opportunity.

Seek the success that awaits the C student in America. The rest of us are depending on you.

ABOUT THE AUTHOR

Luke Pickett grew up on Woodford's Corner in Portland, Maine. He is a graduate of Cheverus High School in Portland and Georgetown University in Washington, D.C. with a degree in economics. Luke has worked in the commercial real estate industry his entire career with companies such as Chase, Crow Holdings and CB Richard Ellis. He has studied the American education system for many years, and currently sits on his local school board. Luke resides in Stratham, New Hampshire with his wife Anne and four children.

INDEX

Made in the USA
Charleston, SC
27 May 2011